THE CERTIFIC...

MW00909630

Small Boat Level 1
Instructor Manual

Your guide to preparing for and running effective sailing classes.

Published by the United States Sailing Association
1 Roger Williams University Way, Bristol, RI 02809
www.ussailing.org

Acknowledgements
This book has been created by our talented team of designers, illustrators, photographers and writers. Invaluable input and advice were provided by the following subject matter experts who generously volunteered their time to the project: Steve Maddox, Kim Hapgood, Rob Hurd and Jane Millman. US Sailing staff contributed to this project as follows: Jen Guimaraes, Youth Education Manager; Janel Zarkowski, Siebel Sailors Program Coach; Meredith Dart, Siebel Sailors Program Coach; Blair Overman, Siebel Sailors Program Manager; Stu Gilfillen, Education Director; Peri Burns, Educational Operations Manager; Bradley Schoch, Senior Instructional Designer; Jessica Servis, Project Manager. Photography by Belle Stachan and Preston Anderson.

The National Standard for Quality Sailing Instruction

CONTENTS

ABC TEACHING BEGINNERS (continued)

ON-WATER PRACTICE   74

INSTRUCTOR TOOLBOX   87

ⓘ INTRODUCTION

Welcome to the world of teaching sailing! You will find the role of being a teacher quite different from being a sailor or a student. Teaching can be challenging and demanding, but you will receive a great amount of satisfaction and happiness from teaching others how to sail.

Beginners offer the greatest challenge and the greatest reward. They learn a large volume in a very short period of time. One week they have never seen a sailboat; the next week they are sailing it by themselves, demonstrating the success of your role as an instructor. Your beginner students will never see the same rapid rate of progress again in their sailing careers, because from that point on these students will be building on the skills they have already acquired.

National Certification System

The Small Boat Sailor Skill Levels focus on building a strong command of basic sailing skills at a developmentally appropriate age nationwide. The focus is to strengthen each sailor's foundational skills and then build incrementally and sequectially through Intemediate, and Advanced skill books. When students have mastered the foundational skills they can then begin to either learn how to race and potentially move to high performance sailing such as foiling.

As instructors, it is your responsibility to document your students' progress and check off each skill in the *Small Boat Beginner Sailor Certification Record Book* or the Skill Up app as your students complete them. When all the beginner skills are completed, the student may send the book to US Sailing with proper payment. They will then receive the *Official Logbook of Sailing*, with added cerification stickers, which certifies them as a US Sailing Small Boat Sailor. This record of sailing accomplishment will be beneficial when students want to charter sailboats, obtain a U.S. Coast Guard license, meet state education and/or licensing requirements, become a race official or sailing judge, and document their skills beyond courses, races and experience.

Small Boat Sailor Certification System

Generally, small boats are under 25 feet in length. They include a wide assortment of dinghies, daysailers, multihulls, and small keelboats. Because of their size and simplicity, many small sailboats can be sailed by just one or two people.

- ▶ **Small Boat Beginner Sailor** - Sailor should be able to sail out and back with a friend in a wide-open space.
- ▶ **Small Boat Intermediate Sailor** - Sailor should be able to sail out and back by themselves or with a friend in a more confined space.
- ▶ **Small Boat Advanced Sailor** - Sailor should be able to sail in a confined space by themselves.

The US Sailing Small Boat Sailor Certification System provides a structured learning path for you to follow as you develop your sailing skills. Whether you sail dinghies or keelboats, you will find plenty of opportunities to establish and continue building your sailing credentials. By acquiring this Certification Record Book, you have taken an important first step in documenting your sailing skills. similar setup and/or isolate the same or similar skills.

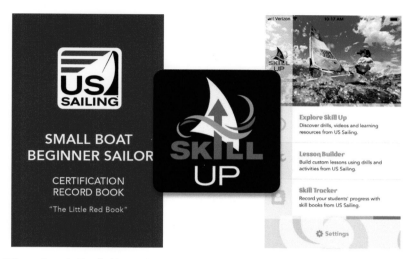

Physical Publication   Digital App

Responsibilities of a US Sailing Instructor

As a professional, you are responsible to your students, their parents, your employer and co-workers, US Sailing and yourself. The degree to which you live up to those responsibilities largely determines your level of professionalism.

1. Responsibility to your students:

▶ **Safety:** You have a legal duty and a personal responsibility to try to anticipate danger and protect students from it. You are responsible for taking charge of all facets of the learning environment and maintaining sufficient control of it so that nobody gets hurt.

▶ **Fun:** Whatever style of sailing your various students aspire to, one thing they have in common is a desire for boating. Today most people boat for fun. One of the first and most common questions friends and family ask after class is, *"Was it fun?"*

▶ **Learning:** You succeed when your students learn. Start by memorizing students' names or use name tags to help break the ice and begin team building.

2. Responsibility to US Sailing:

Once you become certified, you represent US Sailing and reflect its standards every time you teach sailing. Among your primary professional responsibilities is a duty to US Sailing and your fellow certified instructors to live up to the standards of your certification credential.

You must keep the following up-to-date:
- ▶ US Sailing Membership
- ▶ Instructor Certification
- ▶ First Aid
- ▶ CPR
- ▶ SafeSport

3. Responsibility to Yourself:

To be fair to yourself and all those who rely on you, you need to stay healthy, alert, positive and focused.

Attributes of a US Sailing Instructor

(Personal & Professional Skill Rubric from Level 1 Instructor Course)

- ▶ **Punctuality** - Arrives well in advance.
- ▶ **Professional Appearance** - Is dressed appropriately, wears closed-toed shoes and presents themself in a professional way throughout the course.
- ▶ **Effort/ Preparation** - Is well-prepared for all presentations and evaluations.
- ▶ **Professional Conduct** - Presents self in a safe and professional way; prepares; takes seriously the material covered; is attentive to and respectful of students and other coaches and instructors.
- ▶ **Open Minded** - Is totally open to and embraces alternative approaches and differences of opinion.
- ▶ **Positive Attitude** - Always demonstrates through word and actions a positive attitude throughout the course.
- ▶ **Equipment Management** - Demonstrates a high degree of respect for equipment, facility and the environment.
- ▶ **Leadership Skills** - Takes initiative and motivates others to act in a professional manner through actions and/or words.
- ▶ **Participation in Discussion** - Is always prepared, participates actively and contributions reflect understanding of the material on multiple levels.
- ▶ **Collaboration Skills (Team Player)** - Works well with others, shares ideas/ insights, supports other ICs in their efforts and provides meaningful feedback throughout the course.

5 STAGES TO A BETTER SPORT EXPERIENCE

STAGE 5
Thrive & Mentor
Age: For Life
(Being Active for Life)
5

STAGE 4
Excel for High Performance
Age: 15+
Athletic Experience: 10+ yrs

STAGE 4
Participate & Succeed
Age: 15+
Athletic Experience: 10+ yrs
4

STAGE 3
Train & Compete
Age: 13 - 19
Athletic Experience: 6 - 10 yrs
3

STAGE 2
Develop & Challenge
Age: 10 - 16
Athletic Experience: 3 - 6 yrs
2

STAGE 1
Discover, Learn & Play
Age: 0 - 12
Athletic Experience: 1 - 3 yrs
1

American Development Model (ADM)[1]

Our goal at US Sailing is to build lifetime boaters. All sports see participants drop out over time. Let's ensure we start with a positive experience for your youth.

USA Hockey developed and instituted the American Development Model (ADM) in 2009. The United States Olympic & Paralympic Committee partnered with the NGB to adopt and adapt the model for Team USA in 2014 to help Americans realize their full athletic potential and utilize sport as a path toward an active and healthy lifestyle.

Using ADM, US Sailing has outlined key points sailing instructors should consider and be aware of when crafting programs to create a positive youth experience:

- ▶ **Emotional development** - The ability to regulate one's own emotions and manage successful interactions with other people.
- ▶ **Cognitive development** - The growth of a child's ability to think and reason.
- ▶ **Physical development** - Physical development includes both growth and the ability to use muscles and body parts for particular skills.

These developmental milestones should inform how you craft the duration and complexity of the following sailing activities:

- ▶ Instructional Sessions (chalk talks, land drills and water drills)
- ▶ Practice Sessions (on the water)
- ▶ Games (on land and on the water)
- ▶ Competitions
- ▶ Boat type
- ▶ Marine environment (wind, weather, current, tides, etc.)

Excellence takes time, please consider the importance of fundamentals as you start working with beginners and build training that is appropriate for their progression throughout the sport. Remember the goal is to retain your students so they can enjoy the sport for a lifetime.

1 American Development Model, Team USA [website], https://www.teamusa.org/About-the-USOPC/Coaching-Education/American-Development-Model, (accessed February 7, 2022)

Sustainability in Sport

In our sport, our field is the ocean. So, we are ALL responsible for environmental stewardship. Coaches, instructors, race officials, parents, volunteers and sailors all play a role in maintaining a safe and sustainable environment.

There are four practices to the sailor's role in environmental stewardship and sustainability.

▶ **Role Model** - Just like wearing a life jacket, a coach should model refuse, reduce, reuse and recycle.

▶ **Refuse/ Reduce** - Refuse single-use plastics by using a reusable water bottle and replacing zipper seal bags and plastic silverware with reusable food containers or beeswax food wraps.

▶ **Use** - Choose eco-friendly products for clean up, wash downs, boat operations maintenance and storage options.

▶ **Provide** - Make water refill and recycling stations available at your facility and on the water.

Link to Sailors for the Sea: https://www.sailorsforthesea.org/
Link to Sustainability Guide for Sailing Centers : http://content.yudu.com/web/2vwiu/0A2vwiv/SustainabilityGuide/html/index.html

Notes

 # SAFETY

Life Jacket Check Guidelines

As a sailing instructor, one of your primary responsibilities is safety. First, check that your personal life jacket is U.S. Coast Guard approved, properly fits, and is buckled or zipped. Next, it is your responsibility to teach your students how to select a life jacket, how to make sure it fits properly, and when to wear it.

Some tips from the National Safe Boating Council when conducting life jacket checks for your sailors:

- ▶ Check the manufacturer's ratings for your size and weight.
- ▶ Make sure the life jacket is properly zipped and/or buckled.
- ▶ Check for fit by raising your arms above your head while wearing the life jacket and ask a friend to grasp the tops of the arm openings and gently pull up.
- ▶ Ensure your life jacket fits properly with no excess room above the openings and the life jacket does not ride up over your chin or face.
- ▶ Life jackets that are too big will cause the flotation device to push up around your face, which could be dangerous.
- ▶ Life jackets that are too small may not be able to keep you afloat.

Water Comfort Check Guidelines
In-Person Level 1 Course & Students

The purpose of the US Sailing Water Comfort Check is to determine a person's comfort level in the water, not their swimming ability. At the in-person portion of your Small Boat Level 1 Instructor Course you will need to demonstrate your comfort in the water before participating in any on-water activities including sailing and capsize recovery.

US Sailing recommends that after you become a certified Small Boat Level 1 Instructor, you use the same process to assess water comfort in your students back at your sailing organization. Everyone must wear a U.S. Coast Guard approved, properly fitted, life jacket during the entirety of the water comfort check.

Life Jacket Fit?

Jump In

25 Yards Swim

1 Min. Tread

There are several ways to conduct a water comfort check, and the American Red Cross[1] and US Sailing recommend this sequence of critical water safety skills:

1. Dress appropriately to participate in the water comfort check, wear a drysuit or wetsuit if needed for cold weather days.
2. Select and put on a properly fitting U.S. Coast Guard approved life jacket.
3. Step or jump into the water over your head.
4. Return to the surface and float or tread water for one minute.
5. Swim 25 yards parallel to the dock, if possible.
6. Exit from the water.

Items to Consider When Conducting a Water Comfort Check

▶ It is your responsibility as the instructor to select a safe location for the Water Comfort Check. It can be performed in the body of water where you sail, off a dock, off a beach, or in a pool.

▶ Find out if your site requires that a lifeguard be on duty.

▶ Check for any safety hazards or submerged objects in the swim area and consider the water quality and temperature.

▶ Have flotation rescue equipment nearby and ready for use such as a throw ring, lifeguard rescue tube or can.

▶ As the instructor, you must be within rescue distance at all times during the swim check.

▶ Have one to two students in the water at a time, unless there are additional instructors to supervise.

▶ Consider the risks of stray electrical current in the water if Water Comfort Check if administered near the docks that have power on them.

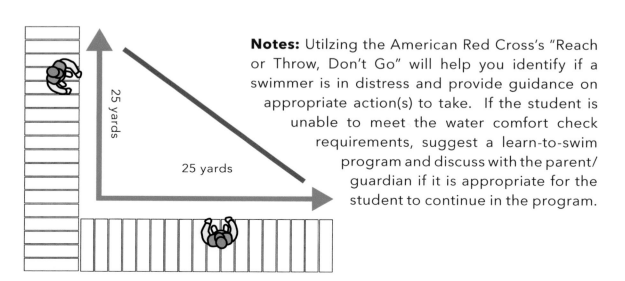

25 yards

25 yards

Notes: Utilzing the American Red Cross's "Reach or Throw, Don't Go" will help you identify if a swimmer is in distress and provide guidance on appropriate action(s) to take. If the student is unable to meet the water comfort check requirements, suggest a learn-to-swim program and discuss with the parent/guardian if it is appropriate for the student to continue in the program.

1 American Red Cross [website], https://www.redcross.org/take-a-class/swimming/centennial, (accessed Feb 7, 2022)

Wind and Weather Awareness

It is important that your students learn to appreciate the forces of wind and water. Make them aware that the sailing environment and sea state can often change quickly and contain a variety of different variables, like water and air temperative, waves, current, wind, clouds, storms, etc. Even a beautiful sunny day can rapidly deteriorate into bad weather.

Starting with the first lesson, you should help your students develop their observational skills so they can anticipate and "see" these changes. At the same time, make them aware of how these observations, combined with a weather forecast and a knowledge of their sailing limitations, will help them determine whether it's safe to go sailing and when to return to shore.

Reinforce throughout the course that environmental awareness calls for continuous observation of the wind, weather, water conditions, current and distance from the shore.

Dress Properly for Sailing

Clothes worn for sailing should be layered. Recommended fabrics include those that dry quickly and are UV resistant and include SPF coverage. Lighter colors reflect heat and dark colors absorb heat. Point out the importance of wearing clothing that allows a full range of motion in wet or dry conditions.

It is important to choose sunscreens with an SPF of 30 or higher that protect against a wide range of both UVB and UVA rays. These will provide protection from both direct sunlight and sunlight reflected off the water. Even on cloudy days, some ultraviolet rays penetrate the clouds and can damage the skin and eyes. The risks of overexposure include skin cancer, premature aging, and other skin problems.

Hot days call for a light-colored hat or visor with a dark color under the bill to minimize the reflection of sunlight. Urge students to wear quality sunglasses with ultraviolet protection.

This will reduce the possibility of developing eye damage. On windy days, sunglasses also keep salt and water out of our eyes. Don't forget to have a strap for your sunglasses or they may go overboard. For wet and cold weather, waterproof boots with wool or synthetic socks will keep feet warm and dry. Water shoes or sneakers are other options for footwear. Properly fitting foul weather gear is key for wet and cold days. There are times when gloves may be desirable.

Daily Safety Reminders

▶ Everyone must wear a properly fitting U.S. Coast Guard-approved life jacket.

▶ Wear shoes with nonskid soles.

▶ Listen to marine forecasts and check the sky to avoid the heavy winds that can cause accidents.

▶ Move carefully and use one hand for yourself and one for the boat.

▶ Sailors should be aware of the boom at all times to avoid accidental contact.

▶ Brief inexperienced guests and crew about the boat's safe and danger zones, especially the boom during a jibe.

▶ Be familiar with the appropriate overboard recovery procedures for the boat being sailed.

▶ All instructors must follow safe powerboat guidelines in the evaluation criteria for this instructor certification course at all times.

▶ Keep a close eye out for who's struggling or uncomfortable in the water.

Executing an Overboard Rescue

Someone or something may fall in the water while the boat is sailing. We refer to this as and overboard rescue. The goal throughout the rescue is to get the person, or object, back on board as quickly as possible. Loudly alert "[Crew or Object] overboard!" and keep visual contact with the person or object in the water. Complete a Figure-8 like course and keep the person or object to windward. Details on this maneuver can be found in the Overboard Rescue Lesson Plan. When bringing a person back on board, move to the stern of the boat and lift them into the boat using an underarm grab.

Communication on the Water

A whistle is your loudest option for communicating on the water.

Sailors have to understand what your whistles mean. For example, have some whistle sequences that always mean the same thing (lots of short whistles could mean, look at me).

Using preset hand signals is also a great way to communicate well out on the water. Go over these hand signals before leaving the dock with your sailors during the chalk talk.

Practice your safety signals out on the water before you start your lesson.

Try this drill. Designate a home base and a special sequence of whistles that instructs sailors to go to that base. Inflatable toys (such as a shark, turtle, SpongeBob, etc.) work well. It is a good idea to practice this with your class; in the case of an emergency, you may need to use this drill.

Notes

TEACHING STUDENTS TO SAIL

It's important that you give your students a solid foundation of sailing skills and knowledge. The US Sailing Signature Progression of Learning follows a step-by-step progression that starts with fundamental skills and builds on them. As your students become more accomplished, you will help them build upon their previous experience and introduce new topics that relate to what they've learned in the past.

Lesson Planning

An excellent instructor is completely prepared and has practiced their lesson. They have a clearly written lesson or practice plan.

▶ The objective is clearly articulated in the lesson plan.

▶ The activities of the lesson focus on a specific skill.

▶ Content is presented in a clear and concise way.

▶ Before beginning any lesson, instructors prepare all needed materials for instruction.

These may include:

▶ Lesson plan and instructor notes

▶ Student materials (books, handouts, etc.)

▶ Whiteboard, markers and magnetic boats

▶ Boats (check rigging)

▶ Marks and anchors

▶ Life jackets (for you and your students)

▶ VHF radio

▶ Land drill materials (broomstick, rope, sidewalk chalk)

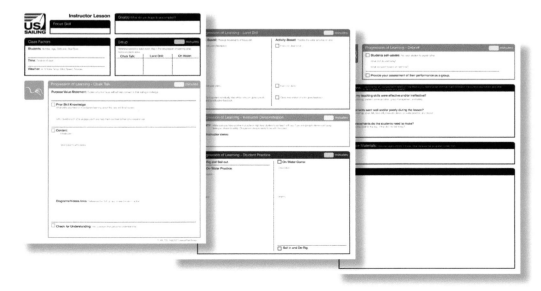

Welcoming Environment

Create a culture where each participant feels welcome, important, and physically, emotionally and socially safe. One of your most important roles as an instructor is to create a safe and welcoming environment where students can learn and play with freedom and activity.

US Sailing Signature Progression of Learning

By implementing US Sailing Signature Progression of Learning as a model in your instruction, you can incorporate multiple pathways and you can strategically minimize lecture time and in turn maximize hands-on skill practice.

Debrief Chalk Talk

US SAILING

Student Practice Land Drill

Instructor Demonstration

 Chalk Talk

At US Sailing and US Powerboating we begin each lesson with a "Chalk Talk," a quick classroom-style presentation. Using their lesson plan as a guide, the instructor should prepare for the chalk talk and be ready to greet their students with a warm welcome when they arrive.

The Chalk Talk has five key components:

1. Objective.
2. Artful questioning.
3. Connecting to prior knowledge and experiences.
4. Activating multiple learning pathways including kinesthetic, visual and auditory strategies.
5. Checking for understanding.

Progression of Learning - Chalk Talk   ___ minutes

Purpose Value Statement: Explain why this focus skill will help connect to their sailing knowledge.

....

☐ **Prior Skill Knowledge:**
What skills you need to know before learning about this new skill (brief review)

Artful Questions (1-2) to engage youth and help them connect to their prior experiences

....

☐ **Content:**
Introduction:

Talking point with detail:

....

☐ **Check for Understanding:** Ask questions that probe for understanding.

Land Drill

Following the Chalk Talk, in which new content was presented to students, the instructor will now move to the land drill where the motor skills are added to the cognitive learning. The instructor should demonstrate the land drill before running the students throught it.

A land drill has five key components:

1. Proper planning and preparation.
2. Providing clear instructions.
3. Making sure the land drill has a direct correlation to what students will practice on the water.
4. 100% participation.
5. Providing positive reinforcement and error correction.

Progression of Learning - Land Drill	minutes
Skill-Based: Physical movements of focus skill. ☐ Instructor description: ☐ Instructor demo. ☐ Each student individually tries while instructor gives specific and constructive feedback.	**Activity-Based:** Practice the water activities on land. ☐ Instructor description: ☐ Instructor demo. ☐ Class tries while instructor gives feedback.

Instructor Demonstration

The instructor models the movements needed to execute the skill the students should be making on the water. One key element is using the equipment in its natural environment.

Model best practices and make your examples clean, clear and methodical. In our example, when demonstrating a tacking drill, it is insufficient to simply tack the boat flawlessly. Rather, you must show and verbalize exactly what you expect from your students step-by-step. Students will better understand exactly what is expected of them once they have seen a strong example provided by the instructor. Instructor demonstrations are not interactive or kinesthetic for the students. The students are only observing, listening and questioning when appropriate.

Instructor demonstration has three key components:
1. Plan.
2. Model best practices.
3. Verbalize your thinking and actions.

Progression of Learning - Instructor Demonstration	minutes
SAFETY - Make sure you have another instructor or high-level student to co-teach with you if you are going to demo a skill away from your students safely. One person always needs to be with the class.	
☐ **Instructor demo:**	

Student Practice

Student practice combines the new content delivered in the chalk talk and the motor skills executed in the land drill with the example provided in the instructor demonstration. This progression of learning prepares the student to practice the new skill on the water.

To maximize student practice time, be prepared. Make sure you have any needed equipment ready to go in your instructor boat or on the water prior to beginning the lesson. The instructor's role during student practice becomes safety, providing positive encouragement and gently correcting undesirable behavior.

The instructor should observe and record each student successfully practicing each skill as defined for the practice session. Notes regarding growth, encouragement and positive developments will be helpful in the next phase, the debrief.

The instructor has four focus areas during student practice:

1. Safety.
2. To ensure each student practices the skill and recieves positive reinforcement and error correction.
3. To observe and record students achieving the skill.
4. Providing positive reinforcement and error correction.

Progression of Learning - Student Practice	minutes
☐ Rig and Sail out.	☐ On-Water Game:
☐ On-Water Practice:	Description:
Description:	
Graphic:	Graphic:
	☐ Sail in and De-Rig.

 Debrief

An essential part of the learning process. It's an opportunity to celebrate growth, give an avenue for questions, close the session and set the stage for future development.

At the conclusion of student practice, instructors should ask their students the following:

▶ *What successes did you have today?*

▶ *What challenges did you face?*

▶ *What do you still need to practice further?*

The debrief is an excellent time for general questions and answers in a group setting. Occasionally a re-teaching will be necessary to help clear up misconceptions or misunderstandings from previous lessons.

Offer praise to the group and call out individual accomplishments. This will continue to build student confidence. You should also use this time to recap the progress made and set the stage for the next class session.

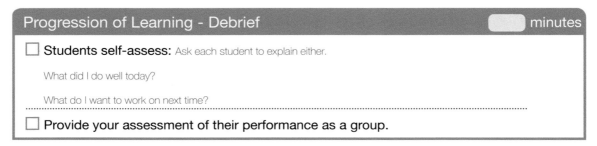

Progression of Learning - Debrief   ☐ minutes

☐ **Students self-assess:** Ask each student to explain either.

    What did I do well today?

    What do I want to work on next time?

☐ Provide your assessment of their performance as a group.

Reflections

Questions that you ask yourself to reflect on how effective your teaching was and how much information the students retained and were able to demonstrate. Did you meet your goal(s)?

▶ *Which of my teaching skills were effective and/or ineffective?*
    Think back to timing, content, communication, group management, and safety.

▶ *Which elements went well and/or poorly during the lesson?*
    Think back to set up, chalk talk, land drill, instructor demo, on-water practice, and debrief.

▶ *What improvements do the students need to make?*
    Think back to the Goal of the day. What did I do well today?

Reference Materials

Titles and page numbers of books, other materials that content was derived from.

Notes

Scope and Sequence Overview

There are components of the Small Boat Student Curriculum Scope & Sequence that you will need to understand: Phases, Focus Skills, and Skill Evaluation Checklists.

▶ A Phase is a set of Focus Skills defined by a specific category. For example, the Phases that are used include Safety, Phase 1 through 3 of Sailing Skills, Theory, and Knots.

▶ A Focus Skill is a targeted skill that a student can complete by demonstrating all the components of the Skill Evaluation Checklist.

▶ The Skill Evaluation Checklist is the observable and measurable knowledge sailors will need to demonstrate that indicates completion of the Focus Skill within the Student Level. For example, in Beginner Sailor Phase 1 Sailing Skills, the Focus Skill *"Understanding Wind"* outlines the following Skill Evaluation Checklist: *"Identify the wind direction; Identify two wind indicators on water; Identify two wind indicators on land."*

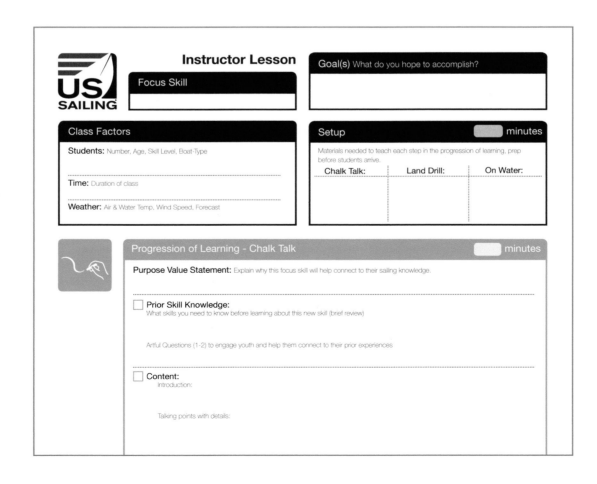

US Sailing Small Boat Beginner Level Skills Lists

BEGINNER SAILOR		
Phase	**Number**	**Focus Skill**
Safety	A	Personal Preparation & Safety
	B	Towing
	C	Capsize Recovery
	D	Overboard Rescue
Phase 1 Sailing Skills	1	Understanding Wind
	2	Parts of the Boat
	3	Parts of Sail & Control Lines
	4	Prepare Boat: Rig & Raise Sails
	5	Stow Boat: Derig & Lower Sails
	6	Launch & Retrieve
	7	Board & Deboard
Phase 2 Sailing Skills	8	Steering with Rudder
	9	Control Speed
	10	Control Heel
	11	Departure & Landing
Phase 3 Sailing Skills	12	Tacking
	13	Getting Out of Irons
	14	Points of Sail
	15	Jibing
	16	Upwind Sailing
	17	Downwind Sailing
Theory	1	Weather Awareness
	2	Water Awareness
	3	Navigation
	4	Rules of the Road
	5	Using a Compass
Knots	1	Figure Eight Knot
	2	Square Knot
	3	Bowline
	4	Cleats

Lesson Plan: Capsize Recovery Scoop Method

Level 1 Instructor Lesson Plan: #1

Focus Skill
Capsize Recovery Scoop Method

Goal(s) What do you hope to accomplish?
The sailors will learn to right a capsized boat safely while scooping their partner into the boat during the righting procedure.

Class Factors

Students: Number, Age, Skill Level, Boat-Type
12 students, ages 12-14, Beginner, Double-handed

Time: Duration of class
Three hours

Weather: Air & Water Temp, Wind Speed, Forecast
80 degrees, 7 knots, Sunny

Setup   15 minutes
Materials needed to teach each step in the progression of learning, prep before students arrive.

Chalk Talk:	Land Drill:	On Water:
• Whiteboard/Markers	• Rigged boat on side on grass.	• 50ft line • Three marks

---

Progression of Learning - Chalk Talk   10 minutes

Purpose Value Statement: Explain why this focus skill will help connect to their sailing knowledge.
When it's windy, or your body weight isn't balanced, your boat can capsize. This skill is imperative to safely recover from a capsize with at least one crew member ending up onboard the boat. It also prevents multiple capsizes.

☐ **Prior Skill Knowledge:**
What skills you need to know before learning about this new skill (brief review)
Swim check completed, parts of the boat.

Artful Questions (1-2) to engage youth and help them connect to their prior experiences
Does everyone know what capsize means? What could contribute to a capsize? How might you prevent one?

☐ **Content:**
Introduction:
There are many methods of recovering your boat and crewmember. Today we are going to learn the Scoop Recovery Method. It is for capsize recovery in a two person sailboat is when the one person is "scooped" into the cockpit of the boat while the other person rights the boat.

Talking point with detail:
Steps to Capsize Recovery (Double-Handed Boats):
1. Communicate - Communicate with your crewmember immediately after capsizing to make sure everyone is ok.
2. Prepare - Make sure the mainsheet and jib sheets are untangled and eased.
3. Swim - One crewmember will swim around the boat to the centerboard.
4. Grab the Hiking Strap - The other crew member will stay near the hiking straps and grab one to be "scooped."
5. Leverage - The crewmember at the end of the centerboard will push down to get the mast out of the water.
6. Upright and "Scooped" - As the boat becomes upright, the crewmember near the hiking straps should hold on tight and get one leg into the boat as they are "scooped."
7. Swim to the Stern - Once the boat is upright, the crewmember near the centerboard swims to the stern of the boat.
8. Recover Crew - The crewmember in the boat will help pull in their crewmember near the stern with an underarm grab.
9. Bail - Continue to bail the remainder of the water out while luffing or starting to sail again.

1. "ARE YOU OK?"

2. Swim around the boat to the centerboard.

3. "ARE YOU READY TO BE SCOOPED?"

"READY"

4. Push down on centerboard. You may need to get on centerboard.

5. Pull in their crewmember near the stern with an underarm grab.

Tips: Three Ways to Prevent Capsizing:
1. Let your sail out quickly so it luffs.
2. Move your body weight quickly to keep the boat flat.
3. Steer the boat closer to the wind to luff the sails more easily.

☐ **Check for Understanding:** Ask questions that probe for understanding.
In what scenarios would the Scoop Method be unsuccessful?
What controls and lines must you be aware of when in the water?

Progression of Learning - Land Drill | 15 minutes

Skill-Based: Physical movements of focus skill.

☐ Instructor description:
Simulate the scoop method on grass using a real boat. Again, emphasize the communication between the skipper and crew. Ask "*Are you okay*?" Loudly respond, "*I am okay*" and give a thumbs up.

☐ Instructor demo.

☐ Each student individually tries while instructor gives specific and constructive feedback.

Activity-Based: Practice the water activities on land.

☐ Instructor description:
Practice the communications used during a capsize between "Scooper" & "Scoopee". Practice steps to scoop recovery on the whistle.

☐ Instructor demo.

☐ Class tries while instructor gives feedback.

Progression of Learning - Instructor Demonstration | 10 minutes

SAFETY - Make sure you have another instructor or high-level student to co-teach with you if you are going to demo a skill away from your students safely. One person always needs to be with the class.

☐ **Instructor demo:**
Tip: This is a great opportunity to have an older volunteer sailor or a junior instructor do the demo.

Progression of Learning - Student Practice | 60 minutes

☐ **Rig and Sail out.**

☐ **On-Water Practice:** Tethered Practice

Description:
Everyone needs to practice a scoop capsize one pair at a time with a bow line tethered to the boat from the dock. The instructor has to make sure everyone can capsize before the entire group goes sailing.

☐ **On-Water Game:** Obstacle Course

Description:
Students will perform a variety of assigned maneuvers at each buoy.

1. Set a course; A triangle, square or diamond will work best.
2. As sailors round each mark, announce specific skills they must perform.

Examples:
"Round mark 1 twice".
"Capsize and recover at mark two".
"Sail backwards from mark three to mark four".

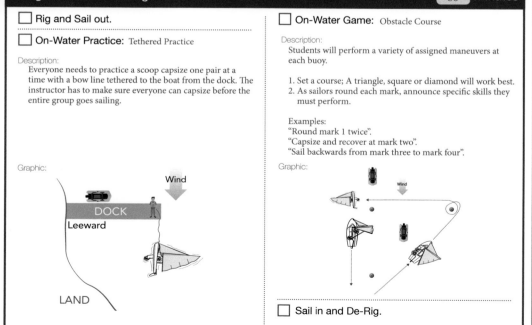

☐ **Sail in and De-Rig.**

Progression of Learning - Debrief   `10` minutes

☐ **Students self-assess:** Ask each student to explain either.

What did I do well today?

What do I want to work on next time?

....

☐ Provide your assessment of their performance as a group.

Reflections: Questions that you ask yourself to reflect on how effective your teaching was and how much information the students retained and were able to demonstrate. Did you meet your goal(s)?

Which of my teaching skills were effective and/or ineffective?
Think back to timing, content, communication, group management, and safety.

Which elements went well and/or poorly during the lesson?
Think back to set up, chalk talk, land drill, instructor demo, on-water practice, and debrief.

What improvements do the students need to make?
Think back to the Goal of the day. What did I do well today?

Reference Materials: Titles and page numbers of books, other materials that you pulled content from.

LSR Beginner, (p. 56), *LSR Intermediate* (p. 46), *Skill Up* App, *Teach Sailing the Fun Way* (p. 26)

Notes:

Notes

Lesson Plan: Overboard Rescue

Level 1 Instructor Lesson Plan: #2

Focus Skill
Overboard Rescue

Goal(s) What do you hope to accomplish?
Students will learn to complete an overboard recovery by alerting those around them and executing the Figure-8 Rescue.

Class Factors

Students: Number, Age, Skill Level, Boat-Type
12 students, Ages 11-14, Beginner, Double-handed

Time: Duration of class
One hour

Weather: Air & Water Temp, Wind Speed, Forecast
Sunny, 8-10 knots, 60 degrees

Setup   15 minutes
Materials needed to teach each step in the progression of learning, prep before students arrive.

Chalk Talk:	Land Drill:	On Water:
• Whiteboard, Red & green markers	• Sidewalk chalk	• Square Floating throwable • Four marks • Whistle

Progression of Learning - Chalk Talk   10 minutes

Purpose Value Statement: Explain why this focus skill will help connect to their sailing knowledge.
Someone, or something, may fall into the water while the boat is sailing. The goal of an overboard rescue is to get the person, or object, back on board as quickly as possible.

☐ **Prior Skill Knowledge:**
What skills you need to know before learning about this new skill (brief review)
Steering with your rudder and controlling speed.

Artful Questions (1-2) to engage youth and help them connect to their prior experiences
Have you ever lost something overboard? If so, what was it?
What did you do when you dropped the item?

☐ **Content:**
Introduction:
After a person or object has fallen into the water, you will need to recover, it or them. The steps to a Figure-8 overboard rescue are: Alert, visual contact, turn, safety position, and finally the rescue. Let's break down each step.

Talking point with detail:
Have students refer to *Learn Sailing Right Beginner* or the demo video in *Skill Up*. Once you walk through the steps, have them trace the figure-8 and stop at each step to verify.

Steps to Figure-8 Rescue:
1. Alert - Loudly alert "*[Crew or Object] Overboard!*" and keep visual contact with the person or object in the water.
2. Sail - Sail approximately 4-6 boat lengths on a beam reach away from the person or object.
3. Turn - Tack and immediately bear off to a broad reach.
4. Approach - Cross over your wake, then head up to a close reach to return to the leeward side of the person or object in the water, making a figure-8-like course.
5. Safety Position - Stop in the safety position within arm's reach of the person or object you're trying to recover on the windward side of your boat.
6. Rescue - Bring the person or object back aboard over the stern using the underarm grab.

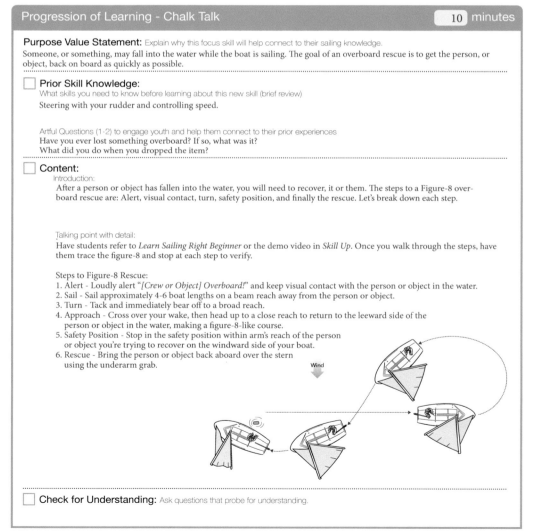

Wind

☐ **Check for Understanding:** Ask questions that probe for understanding.

Progression of Learning - Land Drill | 10 minutes

Skill-Based: Physical movements of focus skill.

☐ Instructor description:
The most important physical movement that each student needs to master is being able to stop their boat on a close reach to leeward of the object or person so they don't run them over. Practice getting into the close reach point of sail and simulate stopping a boat by having students sit in a boat on a dolly. Talk through the factors that affect "glide distance" or the distance your boat will glide over the water once you try to stop it. Factors include: waves, wind, boat type and how fast you can let your sails out.

Activity-Based: Practice the water activities on land.

☐ Instructor description:
Using sidewalk chalk, draw the Figure-8 Rescue Method on pavement, noting the steps in the process. Have the students walk through the Figure-8 and announce each step verbally as they do the physical movements in the step. "Alert, Sail, Turn, Approach, Safety Position, Rescue".

☐ Instructor demo.

☐ Instructor demo.

☐ Each student individually tries while instructor gives specific and constructive feedback.

☐ Class tries while instructor gives feedback.

Progression of Learning - Instructor Demonstration | 5 minutes

SAFETY - Make sure you have another instructor or high-level student to co-teach with you if you are going to demo a skill away from your students safely. One person always needs to be with the class.

☐ **Instructor demo:**
Have an experienced Jr. Instructor complete the Figure-8 Rescue method close to the dock while verbalizing the steps.

Progression of Learning - Student Practice | 60 minutes

☐ Rig and Sail out.

☐ **On-Water Practice:** Person in the Water

Description:
Set up a box with four marks. Call the sail number of the boat that will need to "rescue" the safety cushion. They will enter the box and complete the Figure-8 Rescue Method and retrieve the cushion. Both crew and skipper will work together at first and then try it single handed to simulate a Man Overboard situation.

Graphic:

☐ **On-Water Game:** Whistle Game

Description:
Students will learn basic whistle commands.
1. Decide which maneuvers to include (e.g., tacking, jibing, stopping).
2. Assign each maneuver a number of whistles (e.g., one = tack, two = jibe, etc.).
3. Discuss the differences between maneuvers and which way students need to turn the boat for each one.
4. Arrange boats in a line (follow the leader), with a couple of boat lengths between boats.
5. Blow the whistle to signal a maneuver.
6. Gradually decrease the time between maneuvers to make it more difficult.

Graphic:

☐ Sail in and De-Rig.

Progression of Learning - Debrief   [10] minutes

☐ **Students self-assess:** Ask each student to explain either.

What did I do well today?

What do I want to work on next time?

....

☐ Provide your assessment of their performance as a group.

Reflections: Questions that you ask yourself to reflect on how effective your teaching was and how much information the students retained and were able to demonstrate. Did you meet your goal(s)?

Which of my teaching skills were effective and/or ineffective?
Think back to timing, content, communication, group management, and safety.

Which elements went well and/or poorly during the lesson?
Think back to set up, chalk talk, land drill, instructor demo, on-water practice, and debrief.

What improvements do the students need to make?
Think back to the Goal of the day. What did I do well today?

Reference Materials: Titles and page numbers of books, other materials that you pulled content from.

Skill Up App, *Learn Sailing Right: Beginning Sailing* (p.58), *Teach Sailing the Fun Way* (p. 36)

Notes:

Notes

Lesson Plan: Steer with Rudder

Level 1 Instructor Lesson Plan: #3

Focus Skill
Steer with Rudder

Goal(s) What do you hope to accomplish?
Students will be able to consistently steer a steady course towards a designated target demonstrating proper body position and ability to avoid collisions.

Class Factors

Students: Number, Age, Skill Level, Boat-Type
12 students, ages 8-10, Beginner, Single-handed

Time: Duration of class
Three hours

Weather: Air & Water Temp, Wind Speed, Forecast
Sunny, 10-12 knots, 75 degrees

Setup   10   minutes
Materials needed to teach each step in the progression of learning, prep before students arrive.

Chalk Talk:	Land Drill:	On Water:
• Whiteboard/Markers • Magnetic Boat	• 1-2 Rigged Boats	• Paddles (should be in boats) • Whistle

Progression of Learning - Chalk Talk   10   minutes

Purpose Value Statement: Explain why this focus skill will help connect to their sailing knowledge.
We will learn good body position and how to hold the tiller/mainsheet correctly while steering a steady course and quickly avoiding collisions.

☐ **Prior Skill Knowledge:**
What skills you need to know before learning about this new skill (brief review)
Understanding wind, parts of the boat, board and deboarding a boat.

Artful Questions (1-2) to engage youth and help them connect to their prior experiences
What are the parts of the boat that help us steer the boat?
Where do you sit in your boat so that you can steer freely to the left and to the right?

☐ **Content:**
Introduction:
To steer a sailboat you use a rudder and tiller. You steer with the tiller or tiller extension, but the rudder actually does the work of turning the boat. The rudder can only turn the boat if the boat is moving. If the boat is stopped the boat can not turn.

Talking points with details:
Steps for steering the boat:
• Prepare - Properly adjust your body position, tiller hand, and mainsheet hand.
• Steer - Use the tiller or tiller extension to turn the boat to port and back to starboard.
   • Steering with a tiller is opposite to the direction the boat will turn while moving forward.
   • Move the tiller to the right, the boat turns left.
   • Move the tiller to the left, the boat turns right.

Activity: Use magnetic boats on the white board and take turns have the students predict what happens if the skipper moves the tiller away from them and then towards them.

Diagrams/Videos links: Reference the *Skill Up* app to see this skill in action.

Tip: When sailing, you may hear your instructor say, "Head up." Move the tiller away from you and the bow will turn closer to wind. If you hear your instructor say, "Bear off," move the tiller towards you and the bow will turn away from wind.

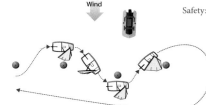
Wind

Safety: To avoid collisions, move the "Tiller Towards Trouble," using just the tiller you can steer away from trouble.

☐ **Check for Understanding:** Ask questions that probe for understanding.
Draw a large outline of two boats on a collision course without a rudder/tiller on the white board. Have students come up and draw the "tiller towards trouble" and a directional arrow for which way the boat will turn to avoid the collision.

Y_SB_024_FEB2022_3SteerWithRudder

Progression of Learning - Land Drill   20-30 minutes

Skill-Based: Physical movements of focus skill.

☐ Instructor description:

Set up a rigged boat secured on dolly on a reach course to keep boom out of the boat.

☐ Instructor demo.

Sit in boat to demonstrate proper body position far enough forward, proper tiller position in front of torso with aft hand, and proper mainsail grip with forward hand. Demonstrate tiller centered to steer straight and moving tiller smoothly side to side to turn. Demonstrate "tiller towards trouble" if trouble is on port side, starboard side, or straight ahead (just pick one).

☐ Each student individually tries while instructor gives specific and constructive feedback.

Activity-Based: Practice the water activities on land.

☐ Instructor description:

Ask students to form a straight line behind the instructor. Instructor walks a wide slalom path to simulate following the leader on the water while instructing students how to use a tiller to stay in line.

☐ Instructor demo.

☐ Class tries while instructor gives feedback.

Progression of Learning - Instructor Demonstration   10 minutes

SAFETY - Make sure you have another instructor or high-level student to co-teach with you if you are going to demo a skill away from your students safely. One person always needs to be with the class.

☐ **Instructor demo:**

The instructor demonstrates steering with a rudder, how to avoid a collision, and proper body and hand positioning in the boat.

Progression of Learning - Student Practice   60 minutes

☐ **Rig and Sail out.**

☐ **On-Water Practice:**

Description:

Blow multiple whistles and announce the safety boat is the "leader" for the follow the leader. Drive the safety boat at the same speed the students can sail in a smooth, wide slalom path until each boat is in line. Have students follow a path the practices steering straight, turning to port, and turning to starboard.

Modification: Change leader to a proficient student for class to follow.

Graphic:

☐ **On-Water Game:** Pladdle Play

Description:

Sailors will learn paddling and steering while participating in a team activity. Note: Boat only no sail hosted.

1. Divide the class into teams of two.
2. Set a mark off the dock that creates a reaching destination.
3. One sailor paddles while the other steers. In smaller dinghies, sailors can also hand paddle.
4. Once each team reaches the buoy, the two sailors should switch places before returning to the dock.

Graphic:

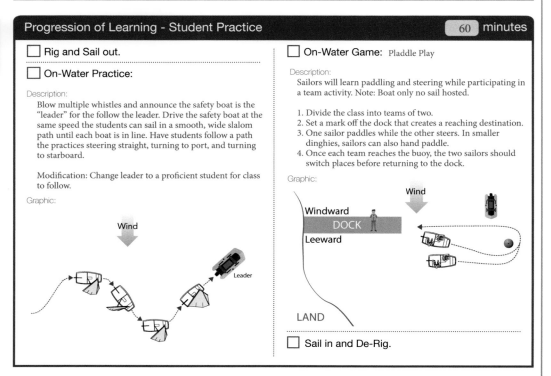

☐ **Sail in and De-Rig.**

Progression of Learning - Debrief

10 minutes

☐ **Students self-assess:** Ask each student to explain either.

What did I do well today?

What do I want to work on next time?

☐ Provide your assessment of their performance as a group.

Reflections: Questions that you ask yourself to reflect on how effective your teaching was and how much information the students retained and were able to demonstrate. Did you meet your goal(s)?

Which of my teaching skills were effective and/or ineffective?
Think back to timing, content, communication, group management, and safety.

Which elements went well and/or poorly during the lesson?
Think back to set up, chalk talk, land drill, instructor demo, on-water practice, and debrief.

What improvements do the students need to make?
Think back to the Goal of the day. What did I do well today?

Reference Materials: Titles and page numbers of books, other materials that you pulled content from.

Skill Up App, *Learn Sailing Right: Beginning Sailing* (p. 20-21), *Teach Sailing the Fun Way* (p. 21)

Notes:

Notes

Lesson Plan: Safety Position (Control Speed)

Level 1 Instructor Lesson Plan: #4

Focus Skill
Safety Position (Control Speed)

Goal(s) What do you hope to accomplish?
Demonstrate how to stop a boat in Safety Position on a close reach and restart a boat to get out of Safety Position on a reach.

Class Factors

Students: Number, Age, Skill Level, Boat-Type
Students: 10 students, ages 8-10, Beginner, Single-handed with Beach Launch

Time: Duration of class
2 hours

Weather: Air & Water Temp, Wind Speed, Forecast
Partly Cloudy, 4-6 knots, 76 degrees

Setup   10 minutes
Materials needed to teach each step in the progression of learning, prep before students arrive.

Chalk Talk:	Land Drill:	On Water:
• Whiteboard/Markers	• Rigged Boat	• Four Marks
• Magnetic Boat	• Four Marks	• Whistle
		• Tennis Balls

Progression of Learning - Chalk Talk   10 minutes

Purpose Value Statement: Explain why this focus skill will help connect to their sailing knowledge.
Sometimes you need to safely bring your boat to a stop while sailing. Today we are going to practice starting and stopping our boats.

☐ **Prior Skill Knowledge:**
What skills you need to know before learning about this new skill (brief review)
Understanding wind and steering with a rudder.

Artful Questions (1-2) to engage youth and help them connect to their prior experiences
We have spent a lot of time talking about how to make our boat go, but how do we think we make it stop if we need to?
What are some reasons you may need to stop your boat?

☐ **Content:**
Introduction:
   Today we will learn how to control your boat speed and utilize the safety position in a single-handed boat.
   Tip: "When in doubt, let it out." - If you get worried or feel like you are going too fast let the sail out.

Talking points with details:
   There are three main strategies for beginners to control their boat speed.

   Step 1 - Slow Down:
   • Let it Out - Grab the mainsheet and let it out. You will see the sail get further and further away from you.
   • Lose Power - As the sail eases the boat will lose power and slow down.

   Step 2 - Go into Safety Position:
   • Look Around - First identify the wind direction and check your surroundings for other boats and hazards.
   • Adjust Course - Steer to a close reach course, ease your sails, and allow them to luff completely.
   • Lose Power - With all the wind spilled out of the sails, the boat will glide to a stop with the boom safely off to the side of the boat..
   • Balance - Adjust your body weight and use small tiller movements to keep the boat flat and on course.

   Step 3 - Speeding Up:
   • Trim In - Grab the mainsheet and pull it towards you using hand over hand.
   • Check the Sail - Your sail should begin to fill with the wind and stop luffing.
   • Adjust Course - Moving the tiller towards you slightly to turn the boat away from the wind.

Diagrams/Videos links: Reference the *Skill Up* app to see this skill in action.

Stop   Start

☐ **Check for Understanding:** Ask questions that probe for understanding.
Have students come up to the board and briefly describe and draw (or with a magnetic boat) how to stop and start their boat.

Progression of Learning - Land Drill
15-20 minutes

Skill-Based: Physical movements of focus skill.

☐ Instructor description:

With a rigged boat secured on a dolly, have each student individually demonstrate how to get in and out of the Safety Position. *Use more than one demo boat for bigger groups.

☐ Instructor demo.
Demonstrate hand movements to slow down, go into safety position and then speeding up.

☐ Each student individually tries while instructor gives specific and constructive feedback.

Activity-Based: Practice the water activities on land.

☐ Instructor description:

Using marks, set up a rectangular zone on land (like you would on the water). Play red light (two short whistles) green light (one long whistle) in slow motion having the students wiggle their arms to demonstrate luffing when they're in safety position on a close reach.

☐ Instructor demo.
Demonstrate playing Red Light, Green Light

☐ Class tries while instructor gives feedback.
Make sure you point out the boundaries of the game on the water (must stay inside four marks).

Progression of Learning - Instructor Demonstration
10 minutes

SAFETY - Make sure you have another instructor or high-level student to co-teach with you if you are going to demo a skill away from your students safely. One person always needs to be with the class.

☐ **Instructor demo:**
The instructor sits in a boat in the water and reviews the proper steps for getting into and out of the Safety Position. Steps: slow down by easing your sail, head up into safety position, and then trim in and pull the tiller towards you to get speed. and sail away.

Progression of Learning - Student Practice
70 minutes

☐ **Rig and Sail out.**

☐ **On-Water Practice:** Stop at each mark

Description:
Use two marks set on a reach course. Students should sail between the two marks. As they approach the mark on a reach they need to slow down by easing the sail and go into Safety Position. Then speed up and head back to the other mark.

Graphic:

☐ **On-Water Game:** Red Light, Green Light.

Description:
• Use four marks to demonstrate the boundaries of the on water practice area. Make sure the sailing area is big enough for boats not to collide.
• One long whistle- yell "Green Light; Start Boat"
• Two short whistles- yell "Red Light; Stop Boat in Safety Position"
• Instructors provide feedback to EVERY sailor.

Graphic:

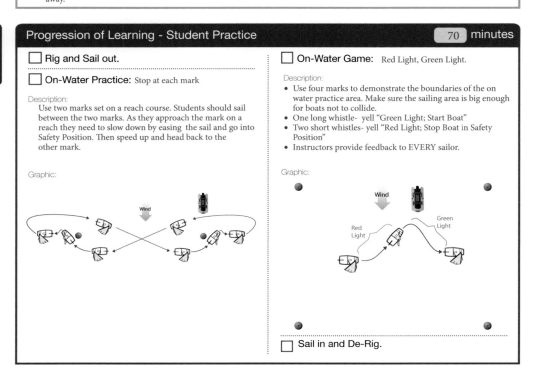

☐ **Sail in and De-Rig.**

Progression of Learning - Debrief | 10 | minutes

☐ **Students self-assess:** Ask each student to explain either.

What did I do well today?

What do I want to work on next time?

☐ Provide your assessment of their performance as a group.

Reflections: Questions that you ask yourself to reflect on how effective your teaching was and how much information the students retained and were able to demonstrate. Did you meet your goal(s)?

Which of my teaching skills were effective and/or ineffective?
Think back to timing, content, communication, group management, and safety.

Which elements went well and/or poorly during the lesson?
Think back to set up, chalk talk, land drill, instructor demo, on-water practice, and debrief.

What improvements do the students need to make?
Think back to the Goal for the day. What did I do well today?

Reference Materials: Titles and page numbers of books, other materials that you pulled content from.

Skill Up App, *Learn Sailing Right: Beginning Sailing* (p. 37)

Notes:

Notes

Lesson Plan: Departure & Landing on Dock

Level 1 Instructor Lesson Plan: #5

Focus Skill
Departure & Landing on Dock

Goal(s) What do you hope to accomplish?
Students will execute a safe and controlled departure from the dock and landing back on the dock considering wind speed, wind direction, current, and traffic on the water.

Class Factors

Students: Number, Age, Skill Level, Boat-Type
Students: 10 students, ages 8-11, Beginner, Single-handed

Time: Duration of class
Two hours

Weather: Air & Water Temp, Wind Speed, Forecast
Sunny, 8-10 knots, 85 degrees

Setup   10 minutes

Materials needed to teach each step in the progression of learning, prep before students arrive.

Chalk Talk:	Land Drill:	On Water:
• Whiteboard/Markers	• Rope	• One Mark
• Magnetic Boat	• One Mark	• Paper & Pencil
		• Clipboard

Progression of Learning - Chalk Talk   15 minutes

Purpose Value Statement: Explain why this focus skill will help connect to their sailing knowledge.
We will learn to carefully depart the dock and slowly land back on the dock with the goal of keeping our boats safe.

☐ **Prior Skill Knowledge:**
What skills you need to know before learning about this new skill (brief review)
Board and deboard, steering with rudder, and controlling speed.

Artful Questions (1-2) to engage youth and help them connect to their prior experiences
What are some factors that we need to consider when we leave the dock?
What are some factors that we need to consider when we come back in?

☐ **Content:**
Introduction:
 Now that you have learned to rig, launch, and board your boat, let's plan for a safe departure and landing from the dock.

Talking points with details:
Departure:
 • Prepare to Depart - Check the wind speed, wind direction, current, and traffic on the water.
 • Depart - Slowly steer away from the dock and trim sails when clear.

Landing:
 • Prepare to Land - Check the wind speed, wind direction, current, and traffic on the water.
 • Land - Approach with sails luffing and stop within one boat length of the landing area.

Diagrams/Videos links: Reference the *Skill Up* app to see this skill in action.

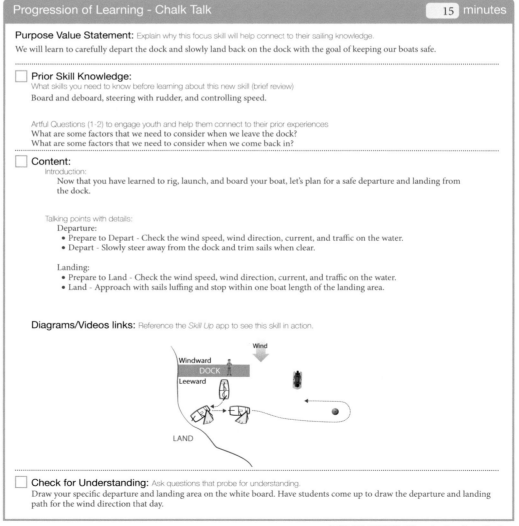

☐ **Check for Understanding:** Ask questions that probe for understanding.
Draw your specific departure and landing area on the white board. Have students come up to draw the departure and landing path for the wind direction that day.

Progression of Learning - Land Drill | 15 minutes

Skill-Based: Physical movements of focus skill.

☐ Instructor description:

The most important physical movement that each student needs to master is being able to stop their boat one boat-length away from the dock with sails luffing to reduce speed and prevent impact.

In a boat on a dolly, have students practice luffing sails simulate stopping a boat from different hypothetical wind directions. Talk through how they would safely approach the dock for a landing in different scenarios.

☐ Instructor demo.

☐ Each student individually tries while instructor gives specific and constructive feedback.

Activity-Based: Practice the water activities on land.

☐ Instructor description:

Arrange a rope to simulate the dock and set up one mark to simulate the mark they will sail around. Have students walk through the steps of departing the dock, sailing to the mark, and then returning to the dock. Instructors highlight changes in trim and rudder movements.

Have students verbalize "Prepare to depart" as they look around and then "Departing" as they slowly steer and then adjust their sails. Repeat the same for landing.

☐ Instructor demo.

☐ Class tries while instructor gives feedback.

Progression of Learning - Instructor Demonstration | 10 minutes

SAFETY - Make sure you have another instructor or high-level student to co-teach with you if are going to demo a skill away from your students safely. One person always needs to be with the class.

☐ Instructor demo:

The instructor demonstrates departing and landing gently and safely on the dock. Verbalize to students "Preparing to depart" as you look around. Then, "Departing" as you slowly steer away and adjust your sails. Repeat for landing.

Progression of Learning - Student Practice | 60 minutes

☐ Rig, launch and tie up to dock.

☐ On-Water Practice:

Description:

Drop a mark a safe distance from the dock on a beam reach to which the students can sail around before returning back to the dock to make a soft landing. Only have one boat practice departing and landing at a time. Have students verbalize "Preparing to depart," and "Departing." Repeat for landing.

Graphic:

☐ On-Water Game: I Spy

Description:

Sailors will embark on a short voyage and log what they find in their sailing area.

1. Create a list of items for students to locate (e.g., birds, fish, floating objects, flags, buoys, trash).
2. Have students sail around and look for the items.
3. Record what they see, either on the boat's deck or in a waterproof notebook.

Graphic:

No graphic

☐ Retrieve boat and de-rig

Progression of Learning - Debrief

`10` minutes

☐ **Students self-assess:** Ask each student to explain either.

What did I do well today?

What do I want to work on next time?

☐ Provide your assessment of their performance as a group.

Reflections: Questions that you ask yourself to reflect on how effective your teaching was and how much information the students retained and were able to demonstrate. Did you meet your goal(s)?

Which of my teaching skills were effective and/or ineffective?
Think back to timing, content, communication, group management, and safety.

Which elements went well and/or poorly during the lesson?
Think back to set up, chalk talk, land drill, instructor demo, on-water practice, and debrief.

What improvements do the students need to make?
Think back to the Goal of the day. What did I do well today?

Reference Materials: Titles and page numbers of books, other materials that you pulled content from.

Skill Up App, *Learn Sailing Right: Beginning Sailing* (p. 30-33), *Teach Sailing the Fun Way* (p. 20)

Notes:

Notes

Lesson Plan: Tacking

Level 1 Instructor Lesson Plan: #6

Focus Skill
Tacking

Goal(s) What do you hope to accomplish?
Learn how to tack by demonstrating the four steps properly.

Class Factors

Students: Number, Age, Skill Level, Boat-Type
12 students, ages 10-12, Beginner, Double-handed

Time: Duration of class
Three hours

Weather: Air & Water Temp, Wind Speed, Forecast
Partially Sunny, 72-degree air temp, 65-degree water temp, 7-9 knots holding steady, storm moving in at 6pm

Setup   10 minutes
Materials needed to teach each step in the progression of learning, prep before students arrive.

Chalk Talk:	Land Drill:	On Water:
• Whiteboard/Markers	• Two marks	• Two marks
• Magnetic Boat	• One long line	
	• Rigged sunfish on a dolly	

Progression of Learning - Chalk Talk   15 minutes

Purpose Value Statement: Explain why this focus skill will help connect to their sailing knowledge.
Tacking allows us to turn and go in the other direction. Tacking is when we change direction by having our bow go through the No-Go Zone.

☐ **Prior Skill Knowledge:**
What skills you need to know before learning about this new skill (brief review)
Parts of the Boat, Wind Direction, Rigging, No-Go Zone, Steering, Collision Avoidance.

Artful Questions (1-2) to engage youth and help them connect to their prior experiences
How do you identify where the wind is coming from?
Can someone explain how to turn the boat using your tiller?

☐ **Content:**
Introduction:
A tack is a maneuver where the boat heads up into the wind until it passes through the wind (also known as the "No-Go Zone") and the wind is blowing over the opposite side of the boat. A tack is one of two ways to turn the boat!
Draw the diagrams of a course for a boat to sail upwind, tacking back and forth through the No-Go Zone.
Let's take a look at what is happening in the boat with the crew & the skipper during each tack.

Talking points with details: Steps to Tacking a Double-handed Boat: Prepare, Turn, Change Sides, & Finish:
Step 1 - Prepare:
• Look - The skipper should look around to check for obstacles and other boats.
• Alert "Ready to Tack" - When clear, the skipper asks the crew, "Ready to tack?"
• Alert "Ready" - The crew grabs both jib sheets. When prepared, the crew responds, "Ready!" If the crew needs more time, they should respond, "Hold!"
• Alert "Tacking" - The skipper should loudly alert those around you by saying, "Tacking!"

Step 2 - Turn:
• Trim In - The skipper should trim in the mainsheet to an upwind course.
• Steer - The skipper should move the tiller smoothly towards the sail to turn through the wind until the sail changes side.
• Jib Cross - The crew watches for the jib to luff as the boat comes through the wind and releases the active jib sheet as it goes slack.

Step 3 - Change Sides:
• Move Body - Both skipper and crew move their bodies to the other side of the boat, facing forwards, while switching sheets and tiller (for skipper) behind their back.

Step 4 - Finish:
• Slide Forward - The skipper will sit down on the new side of the boat, far enough forward so the tiller can move side to side.
• Hands - The skipper switches the mainsheet and tiller to their new hands. Make sure your mainsheet isn't tangled!
• Trim Jib - The crew trims in the new active jib sheet for the new course.
• Balance - Skipper & crew adjust their weight, steering, and sail trim to keep the boat flat.

See diagrams in notes section.

☐ **Check for Understanding:** Ask questions that probe for understanding.
Cover up the steps and ask if anyone can repeat them
When does the boom crossover the boat and what should you do? When do you need to tack?

Progression of Learning - Land Drill | 20 minutes

Skill-Based: Physical movements of focus skill.

☐ Instructor description:

Two benches facing each other; tiller with extension; two pieces of line and a long thin object (to be the boom).

Ask two students to sit side by side on one of the benches as skipper and crew. Have another student hold the rudder at the back of the benches (stern of the boat) and hand the tiller extension to the skipper. Another student stands at the front of the benches holding the broom over the center of the boat to act as the boom. Both skipper and crew hold onto a piece of line to mimic holding a sheet. Ask the students to talk and enact the steps of a tack properly. Switch positions.

☐ Instructor demo.

☐ Each student individually tries while instructor gives specific and constructive feedback.

Activity-Based: Practice the water activities on land.

☐ Instructor description:

Water Drill Set Up on Land: two marks form a figure eight course perpendicular to the wind.

Have students walk through the figure 8 drill and note the steps of tacking together as a group.

Instructors position themselves upwind at a mark to assess each student.

☐ Instructor demo.

☐ Class tries while instructor gives feedback.

Progression of Learning - Instructor Demonstration | 10 minutes

SAFETY - Make sure you have another instructor or high-level student to co-teach with you if you are going to demo a skill away from your students safely. One person always needs to be with the class.

☐ **Instructor demo:**

If you have a co-instructor, one of you can demonstrate a tack on the water, while the other watches the class. Be sure to verbalize all 4 steps to tacking a double-handed boat.

Progression of Learning - Student Practice | 120 minutes

☐ **Rig and Sail out.**

☐ **On-Water Practice:** Figure 8 Drill (45 min)

Description:
- Students will sail a figure-8 tacking course on a beam reach.
- Instructors post up around tack marks to coach through steps and keep a close eye on the potential collision zone in the center of the course.
- Students sail until each person completes three tacks successfully, then switch directions.
- Use the verbal cues of prepare, turn, change sides and finish.

Graphic:

![Figure 8 drill diagram showing Wind direction and boats on a figure-8 course]

☐ **On-Water Game:** Tack Team 30 min

Description:
Divide the boats into two teams (by colors, numbers, etc.) Each team tries to do the greatest number of correct tacks with a fun prize at the end!

Graphic:

No graphic

☐ **Sail in and De-Rig.**

Progression of Learning - Debrief   10 minutes

☐ **Students self-assess:** Ask each student to explain either.

What did I do well today?

What do I want to work on next time?

☐ Provide your assessment of their performance as a group.

Reflections: Questions that you ask yourself to reflect on how effective your teaching was and how much information the students retained and were able to demonstrate. Did you meet your goal(s)?

Which of my teaching skills were effective and/or ineffective?
Think back to timing, content, communication, group management, and safety.

Which elements went well and/or poorly during the lesson?
Think back to set up, chalk talk, land drill, instructor demo, on-water practice, and debrief.

What improvements do the students need to make?
Think back to the Goal of the day. What did I do well today?

Reference Materials: Titles and page numbers of books, other materials that you pulled content from.

Skill Up App, *Learn Sailing Right! Beginner* (p. 3, 39)

Notes:

Chalk Talk Diagrams:
Draw the wind direction, and a boat on a beam reach. Then draw the boat going through a tack and discuss the steps to prepare for and complete a tack.

Draw the Figure-8 Tacking Course.

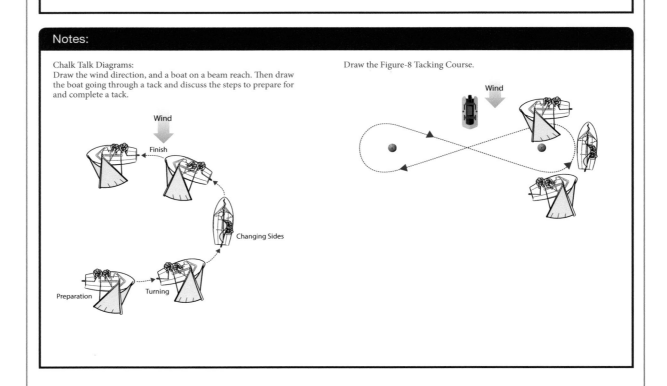

Notes

Lesson Plan: Getting out of Irons

Level 1 Instructor Lesson Plan: #7

Focus Skill
Getting out of Irons

Goal(s) What do you hope to accomplish?
Get out of Irons by; 1. Steer - Move the rudder the way you want to go and hold it there. 2. Ease Sail - Ease the mainsail until luffing to pivot easily. Wait! 3. Sail Away - Center tiller and trim in on a reach to gain speed.

Class Factors
Students: Number, Age, Skill Level, Boat-Type
Students: 6 students, ages 9-12, beginner, single-handed

Time: Duration of class
3 hours

Weather: Air & Water Temp, Wind Speed, Forecast
Cloudy, 6- 8 knots, 72 degrees

Setup   10 minutes
Materials needed to teach each step in the progression of learning, prep before students arrive.

Chalk Talk:	Land Drill:	On Water:
• Whiteboard/Markers	• One Optimist rigged on a dolly	• Three Marks
• Magnetic Boat		

Progression of Learning - Chalk Talk   20 minutes

Purpose Value Statement: Explain why this focus skill will help connect to their sailing knowledge.
Irons describes a boat that has stopped with its bow into the wind and is beginning to move backwards. Being stuck in Irons means you have little to no control over your boat!

☐ **Prior Skill Knowledge:**
What skills you need to know before learning about this new skill (brief review)
Tacking, Controlling Speed, Steering with the Rudder, Understanding Wind, and no-go zone.

Artful Questions (1-2) to engage youth and help them connect to their prior experiences
What does the boat need to turn? How do you turn the boat using the tiller? Where is the wind coming from and how will it affect my boat?

☐ **Content:**
Introduction:
As your boat slows down with the bow into the wind, your rudder will be less effective at turning your boat left and right. Getting stuck in Irons happens to everyone at some point. Today we are going to practice getting out of Irons and regaining forward momentum and control.
Talking points with details:
Diagram suggestion: Show a boat pointed into the wind with sails luffing. Then show the boat moving backwards with the wind. Then show the boat pivoting to be across the wind "getting out of Irons."

Getting out of Irons is broken into three major components: pushing the tiller to one side, easing your sail, then straightening your tiller and sailing away.

1) Steer: Once your boat has stopped, point the tiller the way you want to go and hold it there.
2) Ease: Ease out the sail all the way out.
3) Pivot: The boat will start to pivot onto a reach.
4) Wait: Be patient while the boat pivots.
5) Sail Away: Center your tiller and trim your sail to move forward
        on your new course.

Diagram suggestion: Show each step of a boat getting
        out of Irons using a magnetic boat
        drawing next to each step.

Diagrams/Videos links: Reference the *Skill Up* app to see this skill in action.
Skill Up App Video: *"Getting Out of Irons"*

☐ **Check for Understanding:** Ask questions that probe for understanding.
Cover up the steps and ask if anyone can repeat them? When can you get stuck in Irons? Why does your tiller seem to stop working when you get stuck in Irons?

Progression of Learning - Land Drill   `20` minutes

Skill-Based: Physical movements of focus skill.

☐ Instructor description:

Place a rigged boat on a grass patch where it can pivot easily, could be left on a dolly if needed. Point the rigged boat into the direction of the wind or designated wind direction. Have each sailor hold the tiller and mainsheet standing next to the boat. Have the sailor move the tiller one direction or the other. Then move the boat on the dolly the corresponding way. Have the sailor ease the sail until the instructor pivots the boat to a beam reach toward the same side the tiller is on. Hold the tiller over to one side, have the group count to 5. When the boat has turned and the boom is out over the water, then trim in and sail away.

☐ Instructor demo.

☐ Each student individually tries while instructor gives specific and constructive feedback.

Activity-Based: Practice the water activities on land.

☐ Instructor description:

Place marks on land and have each sailor walk up to the mark into the wind and go through the process of getting out of Irons as they are moving backwards.

☐ Instructor demo.

☐ Class tries while instructor gives feedback.

Progression of Learning - Instructor Demonstration   `10` minutes

SAFETY - Make sure you have another instructor or high-level student to co-teach with you if you are going to demo a skill away from your students safely. One person always needs to be with the class.

☐ **Instructor demo:**

If you have a co-instructor, one of you can demonstrate getting out of Irons on the water, while the other watches the class.

Progression of Learning - Student Practice   `90` minutes

☐ **Rig and Sail out.**

☐ **On-Water Practice:** Figure-8 + Individual Getting out of Irons practice

Description:

Set up figure-8 course for class containment, and one mark outside of the figure-8 a few boat lengths away. While students are doing the figure 8 drill, call over one student at a time to sail up to the mark, practice stopping into the wind, and getting out of Irons near the mark. Once out of Irons, the student can return to the figure 8 course.

Graphic:

☐ **On-Water Game:** Irons to Go!

Description:

When the instructor blows a whistle all the boats point into the no-go zone. Once all the boats have stopped, blow one whistle for right and two whistles for left and the sailors have to get out of the no-go zone to that side. The first one to get their sailboat moving to the correct side wins the game.

Graphic:

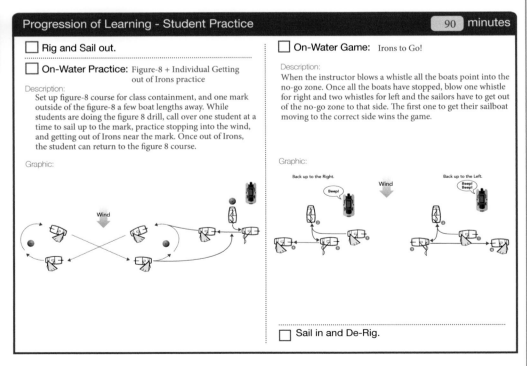

☐ **Sail in and De-Rig.**

Progression of Learning - Debrief

☐ **Students self-assess:** Ask each student to explain either.

What did I do well today?

What do I want to work on next time?

....

☐ Provide your assessment of their performance as a group.

Reflections: Questions that you ask yourself to reflect on how effective your teaching was and how much information the students retained and were able to demonstrate. Did you meet your goal(s)?

Which of my teaching skills were effective and/or ineffective?
Think back to timing, content, communication, group management, and safety.

Which elements went well and/or poorly during the lesson?
Think back to set up, chalk talk, land drill, instructor demo, on-water practice, and debrief.

What improvements do the students need to make?
Think back to the Goal for the day. What did I do well today?

Reference Materials: Titles and page numbers of books, other materials that you pulled content from.

Skill Up App, *Learn Sailing Right: Beginning Sailing* (p. 37), *Learn Sailing Right: Intermediate Sailing* (p. 22)

Notes:

Notes

Lesson Plan: Points of Sail

Level 1 Instructor Lesson Plan: #8

Focus Skill
Points of Sail

Goal(s) What do you hope to accomplish?
Students will demonstrate knowledge of points of sail by identifying the points of sail and demonstrating the proper sail trim and heading on each of the basic points of sail (no-go zone, close-hauled, reach, run).

Class Factors

Students: Number, Age, Skill Level, Boat-Type
12 students, ages 12-15, Beginner, Single-handed

Time: Duration of class
Three hours

Weather: Air & Water Temp, Wind Speed, Forecast
Overcast, 5-8 knots, 65 degrees

Setup   `10` minutes
Materials needed to teach each step in the progression of learning, prep before students arrive.

Chalk Talk:	Land Drill:	On Water:
• Whiteboard/Markers	• Rigged Boat	• Four Marks
• Magnetic Boats	• Four Marks	• Bailers with 4' lines attached

---

Progression of Learning - Chalk Talk   `10` minutes

Purpose Value Statement: Explain why this focus skill will help connect to their sailing knowledge.
We will learn the points of sail (including no-go zone, close hauled, reach, and run) so we can steer the boat in any direction we want to go!

☐ **Prior Skill Knowledge:**
What skills you need to know before learning about this new skill (brief review)
Understanding wind, steering with rudder, controlling speed, controlling heel, and tacking.

Artful Questions (1-2) to engage youth and help them connect to their prior experiences
Is there a direction a boat cannot sail or move forward?
Why can a boat NOT move forward in the no-go zone, but CAN move forward in other directions?

☐ **Content:**
Introduction:
  Wind on the sails can push and even pull the hull through the water. The wind direction determines how to position the sails to keep the boat moving forward. Once you know the wind direction, you can trim the sails for the direction you want to go.

Talking points with details:
  Points of Sail - Identify the basic points of sail:
  • No-Go Zone - Refers to mainsail luffing in the middle of the boat.
  • Sailing Upwind or "Close-Hauled" Refers to when you are sailing along the edges of the "No-Go Zone."
  • Reach - Sailing on Reach - Refers to sailing perpendicular to the direction the wind is blowing.
  • Sailing Downwind or "Run" - Refers to sailing in the same direction as the wind and is also known as a run.

  Sail Placement
  • Upwind - trimmed in tightly
  • Reach - ½ of the way out
  • Downwind - all the way out

Diagrams/Videos links:

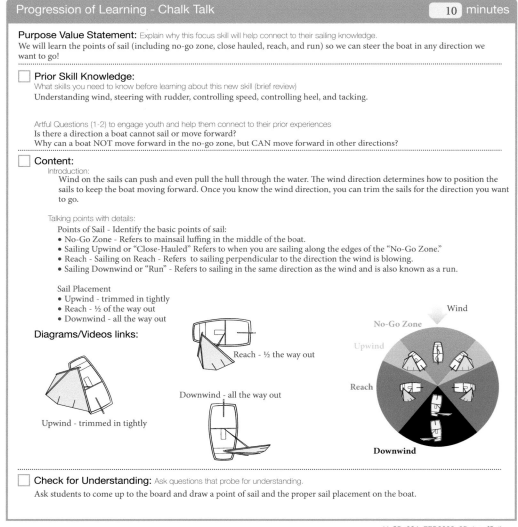

Reach - ½ the way out

Downwind - all the way out

Upwind - trimmed in tightly

☐ **Check for Understanding:** Ask questions that probe for understanding.
Ask students to come up to the board and draw a point of sail and the proper sail placement on the boat.

Progression of Learning - Land Drill [20] minutes

Skill-Based: Physical movements of focus skill.

☐ Instructor description:

Walk through all points of sail with the boat secured to a dolly, trimming sail accordingly, while naming that point of sail. Be sure to use the actual wind direction of that day.

No-Go Zone - Sails luffing over the center of your boat.
Downwind - Ease sails all the way out.
Reach - Trimmed half way out.
Upwind - Trimmed all the way in.

☐ Instructor demo.

☐ Each student individually tries while instructor gives specific and constructive feedback.

Activity-Based: Practice the water activities on land.

☐ Instructor description:

Have students walk the diamond course that they will be doing on the water. Make sure they adjust their arm, acting as the mainsail correctly for the point of sail they are on.

Have students call out the maneuver at each mark and point of sail between each mark of the diamond course.

☐ Instructor demo.

☐ Class tries while instructor gives feedback.

ABC

TEACHING BEGINNERS

Progression of Learning - Instructor Demonstration [10] minutes

SAFETY - Make sure you have another instructor or high-level student to co-teach with you if you are going to demo a skill away from your students safely. One person always needs to be with the class.

☐ **Instructor demo:**

The instructor sits in a boat in the water and demonstrates the proper sail trim for each of the basic points of sail.

Progression of Learning - Student Practice [70] minutes

☐ Rig and Sail out.

☐ On-Water Practice: Diamond course

Description:
Set up a diamond course and have students play follow the leader with one instructor as the leader, demonstrating all points of sail with correct sail trim.

Graphic:

Wind

To Port   To Starboard

1

4   2

3

☐ On-Water Game: Fox and Hounds

Description: Students will practice various points of sail while trying to catch the fox.

1. Choose one student to be the "fox."
2. Have the fox tie a bailer to the transom so that it trails about four feet behind the boat (just like Tail Chasers).
3. Tell the fox to sail away to give a head start.
4. Instruct all the other students (the "hounds") to chase the fox and try to run over the bailer.
5. The first student to run over the bailer becomes the new fox.

Graphic:

Wind

Fox

Hounds

☐ Sail in and De-Rig.

Progression of Learning - Debrief   `10` minutes

☐ **Students self-assess:** Ask each student to explain either.

What did I do well today?

What do I want to work on next time?

☐ Provide your assessment of their performance as a group.

Reflections: Questions that you ask yourself to reflect on how effective your teaching was and how much information the students retained and were able to demonstrate. Did you meet your goal(s)?

Which of my teaching skills were effective and/or ineffective?
Think back to timing, content, communication, group management, and safety.

Which elements went well and/or poorly during the lesson?
Think back to set up, chalk talk, land drill, instructor demo, on-water practice, and debrief.

What improvements do the students need to make?
Think back to the goal for the day. What did I do well today?

Reference Materials: Titles and page numbers of books, other materials that you pulled content from.

Skill Up App, *Learning Sailing Right: Beginning Sailing* (p. 16-19), *Sailing Drills Made Easy* (p. 82), *Teach Sailing the Fun Way* (p. 35).

Notes:

Notes

Lesson Plan: Jibing

Instructor Lesson Plan Level 1: #9

Focus Skill
Jibing

Goal(s) What do you hope to accomplish?
The students will learn to steer the boat through controlled jibes properly by turning smoothly, and steadily, at an appropriate speed, ending on a new course.

Class Factors

Students: Number, Age, Skill Level, Boat-Type
12 students, ages 14-18, Beginner, Double-handed

Time: Duration of class
Three hours

Weather: Air & Water Temp, Wind Speed, Forecast
Sunny, 72 degrees, 10-12 knots

Setup   10 minutes
Materials needed to teach each step in the progression of learning, prep before students arrive.

Chalk Talk:	Land Drill:	On Water:
• Whiteboard/Markers	• Two Benches	• Two marks
• Magnetic Boat	• Tiller with extension	
	• Two Pieces of rope	
	• Broom	

Progression of Learning - Chalk Talk   20 minutes

Purpose Value Statement: Explain why this focus skill will help connect to their sailing knowledge.
When sailing downwind, if you want to change the direction of your boat (which could cause you to pass through the wind), you need to learn how to safely execute a controlled jibe. It's a turn in the opposite direction of a tack.

☐ **Prior Skill Knowledge:**
What skills you need to know before learning about this new skill (brief review)
Wind Direction, Tacking, Points of Sail (POS)

Artful Questions (1-2) to engage youth and help them connect to their prior experiences
How do you put your boat in the broad reach POS position? What do your sails look like? --- Do you need boat speed in order to steer your boat? --- How do you balance your boat in windy conditions?

☐ **Content:**
Introduction:
A jibe is a turn downwind that brings the stern through the wind. During a jibe, the boom moves across the boat from one side to the other. There are four main components to a jibe: prepare, turn, change sides, and finish!

Draw: See Note Section.

Talking point with detail:
Step 1: Prepare
• Look - The skipper and crew should look around to check for obstacles and other boats.
• Alert "*Ready to Jibe*" - The skipper should alert the crew by announcing "*Ready to Jibe.*"
• Alert "*Ready*" - The crew grabs both jib sheets. When prepared, the crew responds, "*Ready!*" If the crew needs more time, they should respond, "*Hold!*"
• Alert "*Jibing*" - The skipper should loudly alert those around you by saying "*Jibing!*" to let people around you know that you are ready to jibe.

Step 2: Turn
• Steer - The skipper will move the tiller smoothly away from the mainsail to turn away from the wind until the sail changes side.
• Trim In - The skipper will trim in the mainsheet to control the swing of the boom as it crosses the boat. The boom will swing fast in a jibe so duck!
• Jib Cross - The crew watches for the jib to collapse as the back of the boat comes through the wind and releases the active jib sheet as it goes slack.

Step 3: Change Sides
• Move Body - Both skipper and crew move their bodies to the other side while facing forwards with eyes looking ahead.

Step 4: Finish
• Slide Forward -The skipper will sit down on the new side, far enough forward so the tiller can move side to side.
• Hands - The skipper switches the mainsheet and tiller behind their back to their new hands. Make sure the mainsheet isn't tangled!
• Trim Jib - The crew trims in the new active jib sheet to the new course.
• Balance - Skipper & crew adjust their weight, steering, and sail trim as needed.

☐ **Check for Understanding:** Ask questions that probe for understanding.
Can anyone share the steps in step 2, turning? (Trim-in, steer, jib cross)
What do you need to say before you get to step two? ("Jibing")

Progression of Learning - Land Drill

30 minutes

Skill-Based: Physical movements of focus skill.

☐ Instructor description:
Ask two students to sit side-by-side on one of the benches as skipper and crew. Have another student hold the rudder at the back of the benches ("the stern") and hand the tiller extension to the skipper. Another student stands at the front of the benches holding the broom over the center of the "boat" to act as the boom. Both skipper and crew hold on to a piece of line to mimic holding a sheet.

Next, ask the students to talk and demonstrate the four steps of a jibe. Once they complete the jibe correctly, they switch positions. If a student makes an error, stop them in the process and ask them to restart, correcting their error.

☐ Instructor demo.

☐ Each student individually tries while instructor gives specific and constructive feedback.

Activity-Based: Practice the water activities on land.

☐ Instructor description:
Have students walk through all the steps in jibing using marks on land. Students can be in a boat on a dolly, which is best for younger sailors.. If students are older and too big to practice in boats on land, have them practice walking through the motions of the jibing while walking ("sailing") a "hot dog" course, using their arms to be sails.

☐ Instructor demo.

☐ Class tries while instructor gives feedback.

Progression of Learning - Instructor Demonstration

10 minutes

SAFETY - Make sure you have another instructor or high-level student to co-teach with you if you are going to demo a skill away from your students safely. One person always needs to be with the class.

☐ **Instructor demo:**
Model and verbalize each step in the jibe using a boat tied to the dock. Practice as the skipper and then as the crew.

Progression of Learning - Student Practice

60 minutes

☐ Rig and Sail out.

☐ On-Water Practice: Hotdog

Description:
Students will sail a "hotdog" course, tacking on one end, sailing on a beam reach, jibing at the other mark and sailing on beam reach back to the first mark to continue practicing. The focus is on the four steps in (jibing mentioned above). Students should continue on the course until they can successfully steer around the course and complete their tacks and jibes at each mark three times in a row. Students will change the drill direction when appropriate.

Graphic:

Wind

☐ On-Water Game: Sharks & Guppies

Description:
Students will improve boat handling skills by trying to tag another sailor with a lightweight ball.

1. Divide sailors into two teams.
2. Give all sailors on one team a ball; they are the sharks.
3. Establish a defined sailing area.
4. On the whistle, both teams enter the sailing area. Sharks attempt to hit guppies by throwing the ball at their sails. If tagged, the guppy becomes a shark.
5. The sailor who stays a guppy the longest is the winner.

Graphic:

☐ Sail in and De-Rig.

Progression of Learning - Debrief   10 minutes

☐ **Students self-assess:** Ask each student to explain either.

    What did I do well today?

    What do I want to work on next time?

☐ Provide your assessment of their performance as a group.

Reflections: Questions that you ask yourself to reflect on how effective your teaching was and how much information the students retained and were able to demonstrate. Did you meet your goal(s)?

Which of my teaching skills were effective and/or ineffective?
Think back to timing, content, communication, group management, and safety.

Which elements went well and/or poorly during the lesson?
Think back to set up, chalk talk, land drill, instructor demo, on-water practice, and debrief.

What improvements do the students need to make?
Think back to the Goal of the day. What did I do well today?

Reference Materials: Titles and page numbers of books, other materials that you pulled content from.

LSR Beginner (p. 43-47), *LSR Intermediate* (p. 34), *Skill Up* App, *Teach Sailing the Fun Way* (p. 29)

Notes:

Draw - Sketch a boat going through a jibe and discuss the steps to prepare for and complete a Jibe.

Draw the "Hotdog" tacking & jibing course.

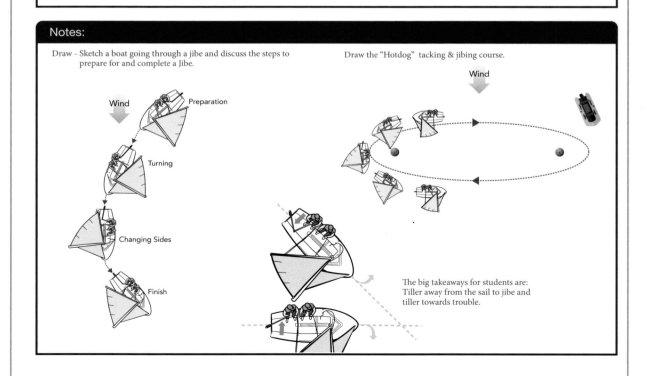

The big takeaways for students are: Tiller away from the sail to jibe and tiller towards trouble.

Notes

Lesson Plan: Upwind Sailing

Level 1 Instructor Lesson Plan: #10

Focus Skill
Upwind Sailing

Goal(s) What do you hope to accomplish?

To be able to sail upwind towards a mark, observing the layline, with proper boat balance on a close hauled course.

Class Factors

Students: Number, Age, Skill Level, Boat-Type
12 Students, ages 10-12, Beginner, Single-handed boats

Time: Duration of class
2.5 hours

Weather: Air & Water Temp, Wind Speed, Forecast
Cloudy, 72 degrees, 6-8 knots

Setup   `10` minutes

Materials needed to teach each step in the progression of learning, prep before students arrive.

Chalk Talk:	Land Drill:	On Water:
• Whiteboard/Markers	• Boat rigged on Dolly	• Three marks
• Magnetic Boat		

Progression of Learning - Chalk Talk   `15` minutes

Purpose Value Statement: Explain why this focus skill will help connect to their sailing knowledge.
If you need to reach a destination upwind, you will need to know how to navigate your boat successfully along an upwind course to get there.

☐ **Prior Skill Knowledge:**
What skills you need to know before learning about this new skill (brief review)
Wind Direction, Steering, Boat Balance, Layline Tacking, Jibing, No-go Zone, Points of Sail

Artful Questions (1-2) to engage youth and help them connect to their prior experiences
Describe how your boat looks when you are sailing a close haul or close reach course?
What happens when you sail too close to the wind?

☐ **Content:**
Introduction:
Sailing upwind is sailing close to the same direction that the wind is coming from. Upwind sailing requires careful coordination between sail trim and steering your boat.

Talking points with details:
Draw a triangle course and discuss how to sail on an upwind leg; including: finding the layline, maintaining a consistent heading, finder proper sail trim, working together to keep the boat flat and keeping the boat out of the No-Go Zone.

The Mechanics of Sailing Upwind:
- Heading: Steer the boat to an upwind course so the wind is coming over the windward side from the direction of the bow. You will be in a Close Haul or Close Reach point of sail.
- Trim In: Trim in your sail anywhere from 1/4 eased to all the way in.
- Body Position: Sit on the windward side with good posture. Sit forward and clear of the tiller.
- Steering: Hold your upwind course by both keeping your sail trimmed in and adjusting your course to keep the sail full.

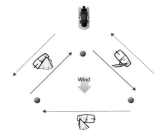

☐ **Check for Understanding:** Ask questions that probe for understanding.
Erase the boat diagrams but keep the triangle course. Ask students to describe the correct points of sail that allow you to sail upwind towards the windward mark, and what the path of this triangle course might look like.

Y_SB_024_FEB2022_10UpwindSailing

Progression of Learning - Land Drill   30 minutes

Skill-Based: Physical movements of focus skill.

☐ Instructor description:

Have each student sit in a boat at the dock or on a dolly and demonstrate proper body, tiller extension, and main-sheet/jib positions for sailing upwind. Repeat the mechanics of upwind sailing - heading, trim-in, and steering.

☐ Instructor demo.

☐ Each student individually tries while instructor gives specific and constructive feedback.

Activity-Based: Practice the water activities on land.

☐ Instructor description:

Set up a triangle course with three marks, clearly identify where the wind is coming from and which is the windward mark. Have the student walk the course in pairs and at each mark ask the students to explain their points of sail and the correct trim for each leg.

☐ Instructor demo.

☐ Class tries while instructor gives feedback.

Progression of Learning - Instructor Demonstration   0 minutes

SAFETY - Make sure you have another instructor or high-level student to co-teach with you if you are going to demo a skill away from your students safely. One person always needs to be with the class.

☐ **Instructor demo:**

Instructor Demo occurred in land drill.

Progression of Learning - Student Practice   60 minutes

☐ Rig and Sail out.

☐ On-Water Practice: Triangle Drill

Description:

Set up three marks as a triangle. Have students sail around the triangle counterclockwise starting from the beam reach and check for proper sail trim. Make sure they adjust their sails, steering and body weight to keep the boat flat.

Graphic:

☐ **On-Water Game:** Sail a Serpent

Description:

Students will join together into sailing "serpents" and adjust boat speed to stay connected.

1. Divide boats into equal-sized groups.
2. Choose a team leader who will begin as the serpent's head.
3. Line up the other boats on the team behind the "head," either by sail number or alphabetically by name.
4. Have each team sail across a designated area while remaining behind the leader.
5. Challenge the teams to create a serpent that stays together in the tightest line.

Graphic:

☐ Sail in and De-Rig.

Progression of Learning - Debrief `10` minutes

☐ **Students self-assess:** Ask each student to explain either.

What did I do well today?

What do I want to work on next time?

☐ Provide your assessment of their performance as a group.

Reflections: Questions that you ask yourself to reflect on how effective your teaching was and how much information the students retained and were able to demonstrate. Did you meet your goal(s)?

Which of my teaching skills were effective and/or ineffective?
Think back to timing, content, communication, group management, and safety.

Which elements went well and/or poorly during the lesson?
Think back to set up, chalk talk, land drill, instructor demo, on-water practice, and debrief.

What improvements do the students need to make?
Think back to the Goal of the day. What did I do well today?

Reference Materials: Titles and page numbers of books, other materials that you pulled content from.

LSR-Beginner (p. 22-24, 36), *LSR-Intermediate* (p. 31-32), *Skill Up* App, *Teach Sailing the Fun Way* (p. 27)

Notes:

Notes

Lesson Plan: Downwind Sailing

Level 1 Instructor Lesson Plan: #11

Focus Skill
Downwind Sailing

Goal(s) What do you hope to accomplish?
To be able to sail downwind, without accidentally jibing while maintaining proper boat balance and sail trim.

Class Factors

Students: Number, Age, Skill Level, Boat-Type
Students: 6 students, ages 9-12, Beginner, Single-handed

Time: Duration of class
3 hours

Weather: Air & Water Temp, Wind Speed, Forecast
Sunny, 6- 8 knots, 72 degrees

Setup   10 minutes

Materials needed to teach each step in the progression of learning, prep before students arrive.

Chalk Talk:	Land Drill:	On Water:
• Whiteboard/Markers • Magnetic Boat	• Rigged Boat on Grass, Carpet or Dolly	• Three Marks • Floating Objects; Tennis Balls, Pool Noodles, Lifejackets, Pool Toys

---

Progression of Learning - Chalk Talk   15 minutes

Purpose Value Statement: Explain why this focus skill will help connect to their sailing knowledge.
If you need to reach a destination downwind, you will need to know how to navigate your boat successfully along a downwind course. Steering and boat balance are really important!

☐ **Prior Skill Knowledge:**
What skills you need to know before learning about this new skill (brief review)
Wind Direction, Parts of the Boat, Steering, Controlling Heel, Jibing, No-Go Zone, Points of Sail, Upwind Sailing

Artful Questions (1-2) to engage youth and help them connect to their prior experiences
How do you keep the boat balanced? If your sail is all the way out, how do you keep your boat balanced?
If you turn left or right while sailing downwind, what happens?

☐ **Content:**
Introduction:
Sailing downwind is sailing away from the direction that the wind is coming from. Downwind sailing requires careful coordination between sail trim and steering your boat. Your boat is being pushed by the wind coming over the stern (the back of the boat). Show Points of Sail Diagram.
Talking points with details:
Mechanics of Sailing Downwind:
- Heading: Steer the boat to a downwind course so the wind is coming over the stern.
- Sail Trim: Ease your sail from ¾ of the way to all the way out.
- Body Position: Sit on the windward side with good posture. Slide slightly further back in the boat, but still clear of the tiller.
- Steering: Hold your downwind course by adjusting your sail trim and your course at the same time.

Tips for Avoiding accidental jibes:
- Avoid turning bow toward the wind, the sail will luff when you do.
- Avoid bearing away from the wind too much, the sail could switch sides very rapidly and jibe.
- Move body weight more towards the centerline of the boat.
- Be mindful of wind shifts and gusts!

Diagrams/Videos links: Reference the *Skill Up* app to see this skill in action.

☐ **Check for Understanding:** Ask questions that probe for understanding.
Erase the boat diagrams but keep the right-triangle course. Ask students to describe the correct points of sail that allow you to sail to each leg of the course (consider labeling marks by color or number).

Progression of Learning - Land Drill | 15 minutes

Skill-Based: Physical movements of focus skill.

☐ Instructor description:

Have each student sit in a boat at the dock or on a dolly and demonstrate proper body position, tiller placement, and mainsheet/jib positions for sailing downwind. Repeat the mechanics of downwind sailing - direction, sail trim, and steering.

☐ Instructor demo.

☐ Each student individually tries while instructor gives specific and constructive feedback.

Activity-Based: Practice the water activities on land.

☐ Instructor description:

Set up a right-triangle course with 3 marks on land, clearly identify where the wind is coming from, which is the windward mark, and which is the leeward mark. Have the students walk the course in pairs and at each mark ask the students to explain their points of sail and the correct trim for each leg.

☐ Instructor demo.

☐ Class tries while instructor gives feedback.

Progression of Learning - Instructor Demonstration | 10 minutes

SAFETY - Make sure you have another instructor or high-level student to co-teach with you if you are going to demo a skill away from your students safely. One person always needs to be with the class.

☐ **Instructor demo:**

The instructor demonstrates sailing downwind using their sails and body weight to adjust the boat, as well as to avoid accidentally jibing.

Progression of Learning - Student Practice | 90 minutes

☐ **Rig and Sail out.**

☐ **On-Water Practice:** Beginner Starboard Triangle

Description:

Set up a right-triangle course with 3 marks. Have students sail downwind and jibe at the right-angle corner. Make the triangle big enough for all boats to sail course without overlapping each other. Make sure students adjust their sails, steering, and body weight to keep the boat balanced and under control.

Graphic:

Tip: Set leeward mark slightly to left so the sailor will not accidentally jibe while sailing on a run. The leeward mark can be moved inline with the windward mark as sailors get more comfortable sailing closer to dead down wind.

☐ **On-Water Game:** Capture the Floaties

Description:

Using a variety of floating objects (balls, pool noodles, lifejackets, pool toys) toss the objects into the water downwind of the group of sailors. On the whistle have the sailors sail downwind and collect as many of the floaties as they can. Once all the objects are picked up, have the sailors sail back up to the starting area and repeat the game.

Graphic:

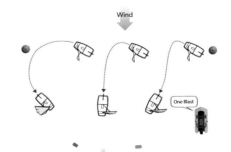

☐ **Sail in and De-Rig.**

Progression of Learning - Debrief

10 minutes

☐ **Students self-assess:** Ask each student to explain either.

What did I do well today?

What do I want to work on next time?

☐ Provide your assessment of their performance as a group.

Reflections: Questions that you ask yourself to reflect on how effective your teaching was and how much information the students retained and were able to demonstrate. Did you meet your goal(s)?

Which of my teaching skills were effective and/or ineffective?
Think back to timing, content, communication, group management, and safety.

Which elements went well and/or poorly during the lesson?
Think back to set up, chalk talk, land drill, instructor demo, on-water practice, and debrief.

What improvements do the students need to make?
Think back to the Goal for the day. What did I do well today?

Reference Materials: Titles and page numbers of books, other materials that you pulled content from.

Skill Up App, *Learn Sailing Right: Beginning Sailing* (p. 42-47), *Learn Sailing Right: Intermediate Sailing* (p. 34-38)

Notes:

Notes

Lesson Plan: Rules of the Road

Level 1 Instructor Lesson Plan: #12

Focus Skill
Rules of the Road

Goal(s) What do you hope to accomplish?
The sailors will successfully be able to identify the stand-on and give-way vessels. They will also learn to always avoid collisions.

Class Factors

Students: Number, Age, Skill Level, Boat-Type
12, Ages 12-14, Beginner, Single-handed

Time: Duration of class
Three hours

Weather: Air & Water Temp, Wind Speed, Forecast
Sunny, 5-7 knots, 65 degrees

Setup   15 minutes

Materials needed to teach each step in the progression of learning, prep before students arrive.

Chalk Talk:	Land Drill:	On Water:
• Whiteboard, Red & green markers	• Two Cones • 12 vessel index cards	• Painter's tape • 12 laminated Cards • Four marks • 12 colored sponges (Two Colors)

Progression of Learning - Chalk Talk   10 minutes

Purpose Value Statement: Explain why this focus skill will help connect to their sailing knowledge.
To avoid collisions you need to know the rules of the road between different boat types on the water. Who needs to avoid and who has "right of way" over another boat.

☐ **Prior Skill Knowledge:**
What skills you need to know before learning about this new skill (brief review)
Parts of the boat and sailing terminology.

Artful Questions (1-2) to engage youth and help them connect to their prior experiences
What other types of boat might you see on the water? Which ones move slower and which ones move faster?
Do some have a harder time changing direction?

☐ **Content:**
Introduction:
When you're out sailing you will need to know how to avoid collisions, identify who should avoid who, and who should keep sailing their course.

In future lessons you will learn additional rules of the road like: when two sailboats meet.

Talking point with detail:
The stand-on vessel is the boat that continues to hold its course and speed. The give-way vessel is the boat that needs to change or alter its course and speed to avoid a collision. Both stand-on and give-way vessels should plan to avoid collisions whenever possible.

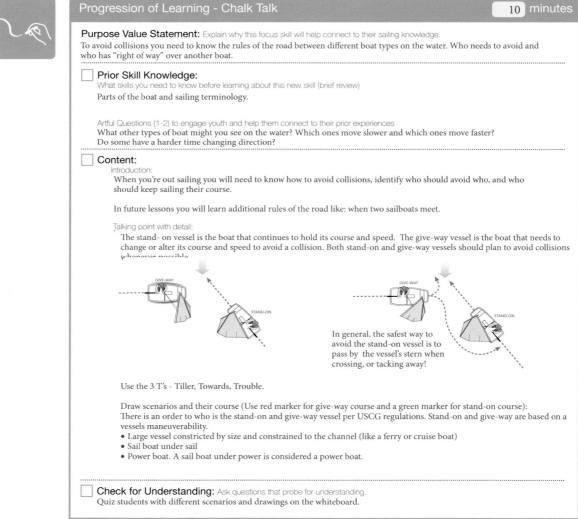

In general, the safest way to avoid the stand-on vessel is to pass by the vessel's stern when crossing, or tacking away!

Use the 3 T's - Tiller, Towards, Trouble.

Draw scenarios and their course (Use red marker for give-way course and a green marker for stand-on course):
There is an order to who is the stand-on and give-way vessel per USCG regulations. Stand-on and give-way are based on a vessels maneuverability.
• Large vessel constricted by size and constrained to the channel (like a ferry or cruise boat)
• Sail boat under sail
• Power boat. A sail boat under power is considered a power boat.

☐ **Check for Understanding:** Ask questions that probe for understanding.
Quiz students with different scenarios and drawings on the whiteboard.

Progression of Learning - Land Drill

Skill-Based: Physical movements of focus skill.

☐ Instructor description:
Create "water traffic" cards that have the names of different boats (Power, Cruising Sailboat, etc) that they may come into contact with on the water. Set up two cones about 10 feet apart. Split the class in half and have them line-up by each cone facing, each other. Split the deck and have them each select a card and announce the type of boat and whether they are stand-on or give-way vessel in the scenario. The students will approach one another on a collision course and either stand-on or give-way. Have student pick a new vessel card after 2-3 passes

Activity-Based: Practice the water activities on land.

☐ Instructor description:
Show colored sponges; set up 4 marks sailing area; describe how to enter and leave sailing area; describe how to pass sponge to next sailor.

☐ Instructor demo.

☐ Each student individually tries while instructor gives specific and constructive feedback.

☐ Instructor demo.

☐ Class tries while instructor gives feedback.

Progression of Learning - Instructor Demonstration

SAFETY - Make sure you have another instructor or high-level student to co-teach with you if you are going to demo a skill away from your students safely. One person always needs to be with the class.

☐ **Instructor demo:**
The instructor should model verbalizing "standing on" and holding the tiller on center line. Then, model verbalizing "giving way" and quickly moving the tiller towards or away from you.

Progression of Learning - Student Practice

☐ Rig and Sail out.

☐ **On-Water Practice:** Stand on or not?

Description:
Create a large box with four marks. Print pictures of different types of boats (Powerboat - red, Cruising Sailboat - green, etc.), and put each type on a color of construction paper and laminate, if possible. Have the students tape their boat card to the boom. Then they can sail in the box and practice standing-on or giving-way to the other vessels. Students should hail "stand-on" or "give-way" on their approach.

Graphic:

☐ **On-Water Game:** Tag you Stand on

Description:
Get a pack of colored sponges (Powerboat - red, Cruising Sailboat - green, Kayak - Blue) Write the type of vessel on each sponge. Students will enter the box from opposing sides with their sponge and act as that vessel hailing "stand-on" or "give-way." They then sail out of the box and toss their sponge to a different sailor.

Graphic:

☐ Sail in and De-Rig.

Progression of Learning - Debrief   `10` minutes

☐ **Students self-assess:** Ask each student to explain either.

What did I do well today?

What do I want to work on next time?

....

☐ Provide your assessment of their performance as a group.

Reflections: Questions that you ask yourself to reflect on how effective your teaching was and how much information the students retained and were able to demonstrate. Did you meet your goal(s)?

Which of my teaching skills were effective and/or ineffective?
Think back to timing, content, communication, group management, and safety.

Which elements went well and/or poorly during the lesson?
Think back to set up, chalk talk, land drill, instructor demo, on-water practice, and debrief.

What improvements do the students need to make?
Think back to the Goal of the day. What did I do well today?

Reference Materials: Titles and page numbers of books, other materials that you pulled content from.

Skill Up App, *Learn Sailing Right Beginner* (p. 53)

Notes:

Notes

ON-WATER PRACTICE

Setting Up On-Water Games and Activities

As a sailing instructor, you will spend the majority of your time each day leading water activities. They give students the opportunity to try a maneuver for the first time, bring their skills together and do what they came to do: sail. Water games and activities follow introductions/chalk talks and usually either a demonstration and/or a land drill. On-water practice has the most variables of all of the teaching methods (i.e., weather, sea state, open space, and that means they require a higher degree of planning and practice to achieve success.

Common mistakes when running water drills include poorly laid out courses, lack of specific directions, students' inability to hear the instructor and lack of group control (resulting in wasted time chasing sailors around). Following are some guidelines to help make your water drills run safely, smoothly and effectively.

Keeping it Fun and Safe

For beginner sailors, have one focus skill for the day; make sure the majority of time within that game or activity will be spent practicing the skill.

For example, if your focus skill is tacking and you set a triangle with a short windward leg and very long reach legs, your sailors will spend only a short time executing tacks compared to a relatively long time sailing on reaches. This may be fun, but it is not helping your students learn tacking in the most efficient way. It would be better to shorten those reach legs so more time is spent going windward.

Assess the complexity; is the skill level and age of your students appropriate for many maneuvers/rules/directions? What conditions do you need for this drill to be successful?

▶ This should be identified in your written lesson plans as a reminder. For example, reinforcing jibing with a jibing slalom with young, first-year sailors would best be done in lighter to moderate air.

▶ Marks close together allow for more maneuvers (tacking and jibing) but also increase the interactions between boats.

▶ Marks farther apart allow more time for students to work on sail trim, body position, keeping the tiller straight, and boat balance.

Will the drill allow you to give sailors feedback?

▶ Some fast action or crowded drills, such as a game of football or the box drill, may require you to stay farther away from the group. If that is the case and you cannot give feedback during the drill, be sure to have a notebook with you to write down your specific comments for each sailor/team.

Will the game or activity allow for good management of the class and their safety on the water?

▶ Courses utilizing several marks (buoys) generally allow for more group control. However, drills such as tacking or jibing on the whistle also give you the ability to control the group; for example, you can have your students all tack away from a channel using this drill. It may be difficult for you to shepherd a group of new sailors out of a mooring field while doing a drill of tacking on the whistle (knowing exactly where they all are in relation to other boats when you signal them), but this drill can give you more group control.

Setup

Maintain group control even while you are setting up. Look around; be sure you have enough space for your sailors to execute what you are asking them to do.

Think about the next drill and practice flow.

▶ For example, if you have a drill that gets you upwind (such as tack on the whistle), plan the following drill so it gets your students back downwind (such as follow the leader or jibe on the whistle).

Execution

Get going as soon as you can and think about pace.

▶ While sailors need some rest, too much downtime can result in people getting bored and sailing away.

▶ Remember that you have a goal skill. For example, if you are running tack on the whistle, you need to blow the whistle often enough so students get in effective tacking practice but not so often that they have trouble getting up to speed before starting the next tack.

Give specific, constructive and positive feedback.

▶ Remember that you are more than just a safety officer. In order to truly be an instructor, you must provide specific and constructive feedback.

▶ Prioritize your feedback by giving the most important first and jotting down other areas of improvement in your notebook. Stay with that boat and observe them as they work on your recommendations. Do not give feedback and then motor away before checking for comprehension and skill correction.

Hand Signals

▶ **Safety Position** - Cross arms overs chest and then spread them wide open. Using the baseball sign "safe."

▶ **Follow Me** - Raise your arm and point back towards the motor of the safety boat. Repeat.

▶ **Circle Me** - Make circles in the air over your head with one arm

▶ **Switch Positions** - Make a fist with both hands and repeatedly bump them together to signal the crew and skipper to switch positions.

▶ **Sheet In or Sheet Out** - Stretch your right hand all the way out and exaggerate the action of grabbing the main sheet or jib sheet and pulling it in or letting in out.

▶ **Okay** - Hold your hand out and above your head and give a thumbs up.

How to Set Marks

▶ Double-check that all knots and attachments are secure. Use an extra locking hitch on bowlines connecting anchor to mark and mark to anchor.

▶ Look around and make sure there is enough space for your course, including bail-out room for sailors; this is especially important in stronger breeze and near jibe and windward marks.

▶ Identify where the wind is coming from by using a wind indicator. You must be stopped for this to be accurate.

▶ Be sure your safety boat is stopped and facing head to wind before lowering the anchor into the water.

▶ Always check that the anchor has hit the bottom (you will feel slack on the line) and then tie a bowline on a bight to be sure that the mark's anchor line goes straight up without much scope (unless it is very windy).

▶ If you are setting a windward/leeward course, start with the leeward mark and then motor directly upwind to your windward mark location.

▶ If you are setting a reach-to-reach course, set one mark, motor to the location of the second mark (in terms of distance), face head to wind. and then motor a short distance to windward of where you want the mark to sit. This allows for your drift back downwind while the anchor is being lowered; the more wind, the more you will drift.

Small Tetrahedron

Small Round Ball

On-Water Courses

Hot Dog

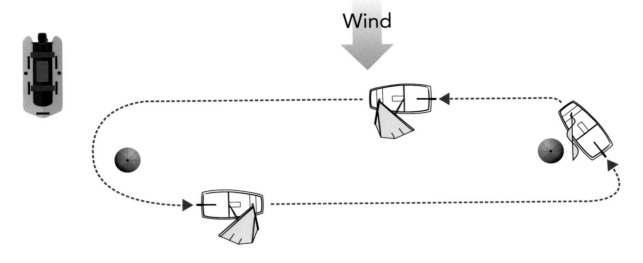

Figure-8

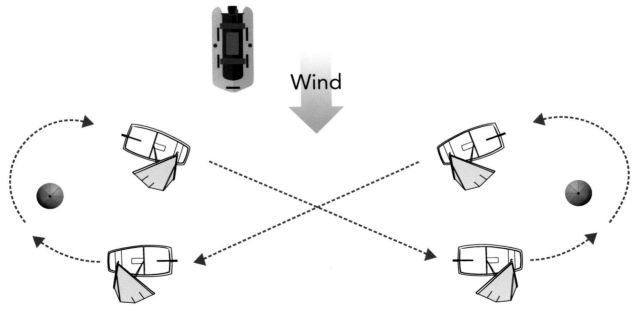

Low Triangle

Wind

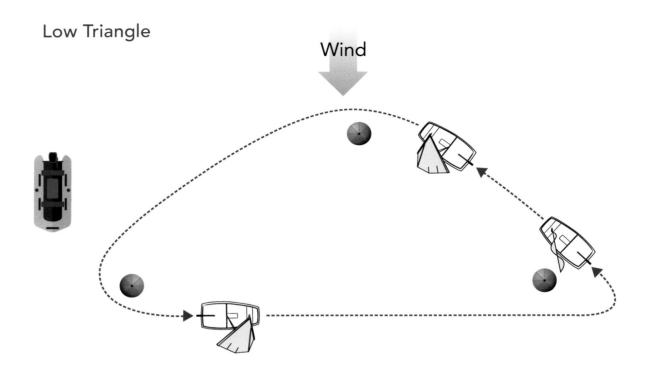

High Triangle

Wind

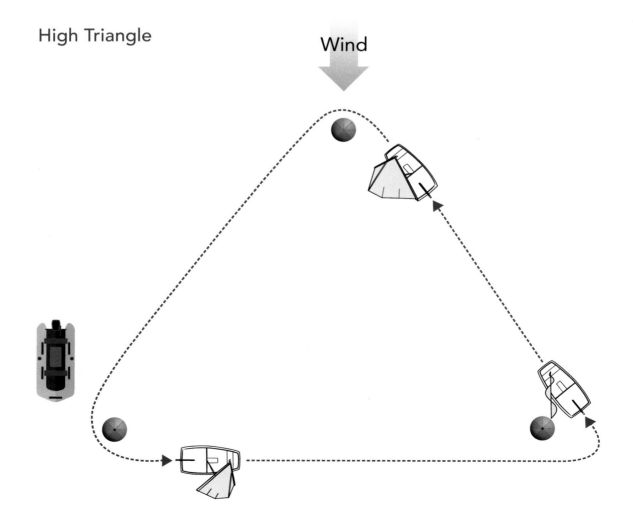

Reach Triangle

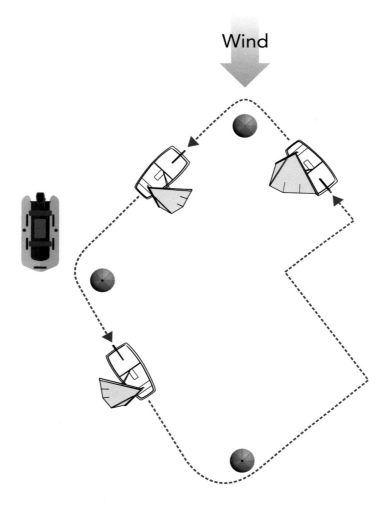

Wind

Downwind Triangle

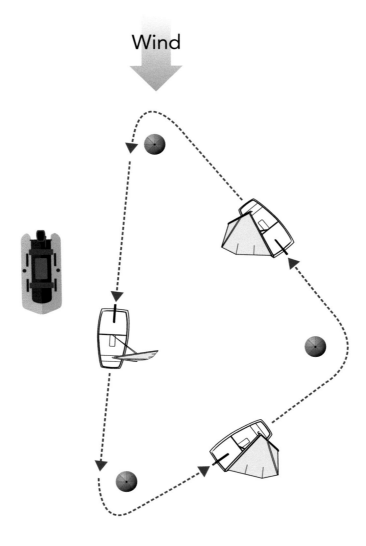

Wind

Windward/Leeward

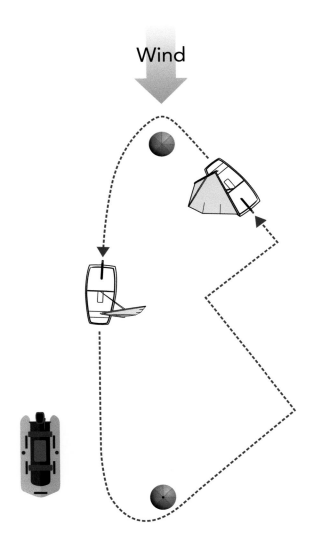

Towing

Factors that Affect Towing

Purpose of the tow: Is it a rescue, an emergency return to shore, or transporting class to and from the sailing area?

▶ Type and number of boats being towed: Are they centerboard or daggerboard dinghies, keelboats or multihulls? Can they be towed without anyone in them, or do they need to be steered?

▶ Type and size of tow boat?

▶ Experience level of sailors?

▶ Wind and sea conditions?

 Towing should only be conducted by instructors with a U.S. Coast Guard towing endorsement or in an emergency situation.

People, Sails and Centerboards

Generally, if a towline cannot be fastened to the bow or led through a bow chock or fairlead, the sailboat has to have someone aboard to steer it and the centerboard or daggerboard should be raised two-thirds or three-quarters to improve tracking. Shifting weight aft to raise the bow also increases tracking. If the boats are not occupied, the centerboards should be fully raised. Sails on dinghies are usually lowered and stowed for a tow. Laser-type sails can be rolled around the mast and secured.

Towing Methods

There are four basic towing methods:

▶ Single-line (bow-to-stern), including a pram variation.

▶ Double-line (bow-to-stern).

▶ Herringbone (V-pattern).

▶ Side tow.

Single-Line Tow

This is a good method for centerboard boats or keelboats.The number of boats on the tow depends on the size and weight of the sailboats and the size, hull type and horsepower of the tow boat. However, a long line of boats reduces the maneuverability of a tow. A separate towline is needed for each boat.

Towlines should be fastened to a strong point (capable of taking the pulling load) on each sailboat, which is usually the mast. To reduce the load on the mast to just that of the boat itself (not the load of all the boats behind it), a double bowline should be used (see detail).

The boats can be occupied or empty, depending on the type of sailboat and how the towline is attached. For instance, Lasers that have their towlines led through the bow fair-leads to the masts can be towed with daggerboards removed and without anyone aboard. The last boat in the tow, however, should have someone aboard to control the tow. With 420s, which don't have bow chocks or fairleads, someone should be in each boat to steer; their weight should be near the stern to raise the bow for better tracking.

The load on Boat A's mast is only that of Boat A and not of any of the boats being towed behind it.

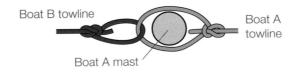

Boat B towline

Boat A towline

Boat A mast

Laser Towing

For towing short distances with the mast stepped, release the boom vang and mainsheet so the sail can "flag" with the wind.

An emergency knot that can be released under load is two turns around the mast followed by two doubled (line is doubled) half-hitches. (A bowline cannot be released under load.)

Pram Variation for Single-Line Tow

Painters (bow lines) should be at least 3½ times the length of the boats being towed. Loops are formed at the end of the painter. Starting with the last boat, painters are led successively through the loop in the painter of the boat ahead. The first boat picked up will be the last boat on the tow line. The loop at the end ot the towline shoudl be a bowline knot. The painter of the last boat is led to the safety boat.

When the safety boat releases the tow, painters come undone like a chain stitch. This is an excellent method to use with young sailors who may have difficulty untying knots that have been tightened by the strain of towing.

Starting with the last boat, painters are led through loops until first pram whose painter is led to the safety boat. Release by safety boat releases all boats - no knots to untie!

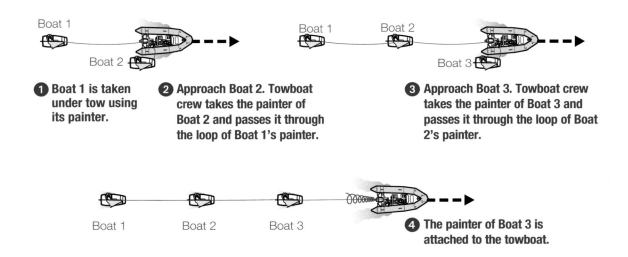

1. **Boat 1 is taken under tow using its painter.**

2. **Approach Boat 2. Towboat crew takes the painter of Boat 2 and passes it through the loop of Boat 1's painter.**

3. **Approach Boat 3. Towboat crew takes the painter of Boat 3 and passes it through the loop of Boat 2's painter.**

4. **The painter of Boat 3 is attached to the towboat.**

Towing details should be adjusted based on boat type. International Optimist Class Rules 4.3b specify, a painter of a single piece of buoyant rope, not less than 5 mm diameter and not less than 8 m long securely fastened to the mast thwart or mast step. When towing Naples Sabots, have sailors pull up the leeboard. When towing unmanned dinghies, take the rudder out and put it in the empty centerboard case to help with tracking.

Towline

Towlines should be inspected frequently to insure they are free of knots and frayed spots. Use 5mm floating line. To improve the maneuverability of the tow boat, the towline should be fastened either to a towing pylon (bit) near the middle of the boat or to a bridle with a quick release fitting.

Towline Communication

Make sure those being towed know the basic hand signals associated with towing, such as come closer, slow down, towline is tied (okay signal), cut/let go the towline, etc.

Picking Up a Tow

Tow boat approaches slowly to the windward side of the sailboat pointed in the same direction.

Throw or hand over the towline, or drag the towline by the sailboat.
When the towline is secured (wait for the okay visual signal), take up slack gently and proceed to the next sailboat.

Maneuvering with a Tow

- ▶ Changes in speed, stopping and starting should be done slowly.
- ▶ Wait until all boats on the tow are moving and towlines are clear before maneuvering.
- ▶ Keep a lookout posted to watch the tow behind you.
- ▶ Keep the towing speed low.
- ▶ Turn in large arcs, using a turning radius approximately equal to the length of the tow.
- ▶ Adjust the towline so the first boat in a line is not being pulled up the backside of a wave (to help reduce load on the tow boat).
- ▶ If a boat falls off, keep the tow moving slowly; don't stop and let the boats bunch up.
- ▶ If conditions are rough, increase control by lengthening the towline or slowing the speed to increase the catenary (droop) of the towline.
- ▶ Remind students of the expected behavior while under tow.
- ▶ Be aware of the possibility of fouling the towline in the propeller.
- ▶ Be aware of the possibility of overhead power lines.

Casting Off a Tow

When sails are raised under tow (which is not recommended for beginners or in windy or rough conditions), the tow boat should head into the wind and move slowly while sails are hoisted. When the sails are up, the tow boat should keep the apparent wind forward of the beam but not in the No-Go Zone. Boats drop off, starting with the last boat on the tow.

Anchoring the tow boat is a slower method, but it provides better control for beginners or rough conditions. The tow boat anchors, sailors then raise their sails and cast off. In light winds, sailors can cast off before their sails are raised and hoist sails while drifting.

Terminology

Initially, the use of sailing terminology should be backed up by the use of everyday terms (e., top, bottom, left, right, rope) until students become familiar with the proper nautical terms. Focus on the basic terms to avoid confusing or overwhelming your students with too much nautical jargon. Learning to sail should be the first emphasis—not learning the jargon. With repetition the correct nautical terms will become part of your students' vocabulary.

An effective teaching technique is to divide the sailboat into two main components: the hull and the rig. Remember that there are different kinds of hulls: monohulls or multihulls (catamarans and trimarans). Each has a different type of underwater foil (centerboards, daggerboards, leeboards, keels, rudders). There are also different types of rigs. Rigs include spars (masts and booms), rigging (standing and running) and sails.

Underwater Foils

Describe the keel, centerboard, daggerboard, rudder or leeboards. Demonstrate how the tiller and rudder are moved from side to side to steer the boat. Keep your explanation simple and emphasize the basic concepts of tiller steering.

Below are Key Points to Emphasize

▶ The boat has to be moving forward (or backward) for the steering system to operate.
▶ Move the tiller in the opposite direction you want the boat to go.
▶ The centerboard or daggerboard, as well as the rudder, needs to be in the fully down position.

Save your explanations about the interaction of the underwater foils, tiller, rudder and water flow for a later time—after your students have had an opportunity to steer and sail the boat. Mention that when a sailboat turns, its pivot point is approximately in the middle of the boat. A good time to demonstrate this is when you depart from a dock or slip. Make your students aware that if they turn one end of the boat away from the dock, the other end turns into the dock.

Know the Boats and Equipment

It is very tempting to try to cover an immense amount of information at the very start of a learn-to-sail class. Instead, concentrate on the subjects that will relate to the students' first sail. Identify the basic parts and equipment of the hull and rig, give a brief description of their function, and demonstrate proper usage.

Use the handouts on the following page to help your students practice learning the parts of the boat. Learning the parts of the boat is essential to mastering beginner level sailing skills.

Notes

Club 420

Name:_____

Label the boat with the name of the corresponding part.

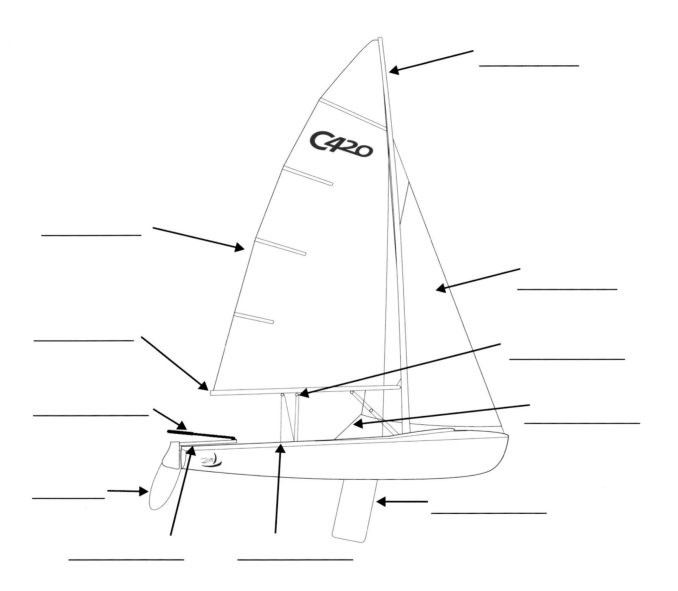

Word Key

Block	Jib Sheet	Rudder
Boom	Mainsail	Tiller Extenstion
Centerboard	Mainsheet	
Jib Sail	Mast	

Club 420 Answer Sheet

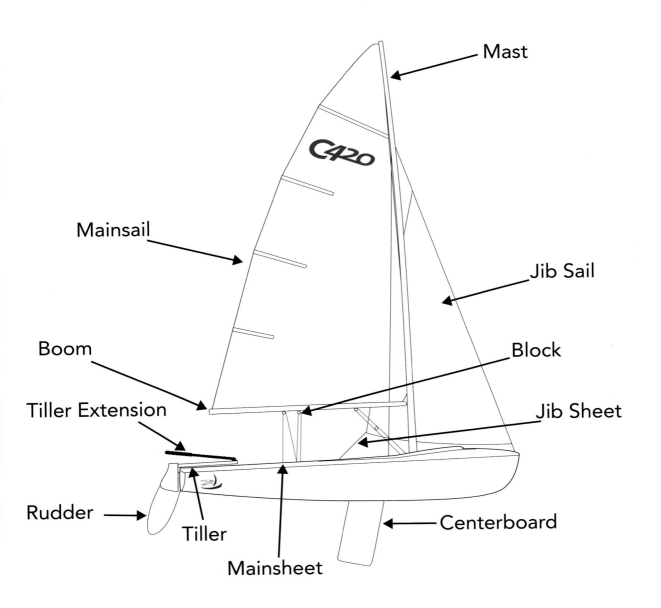

Mast

Mainsail

Jib Sail

Boom

Block

Tiller Extension

Jib Sheet

Rudder

Tiller

Centerboard

Mainsheet

Optimist

Name:_____

Label the boat with the name of the corresponding part.

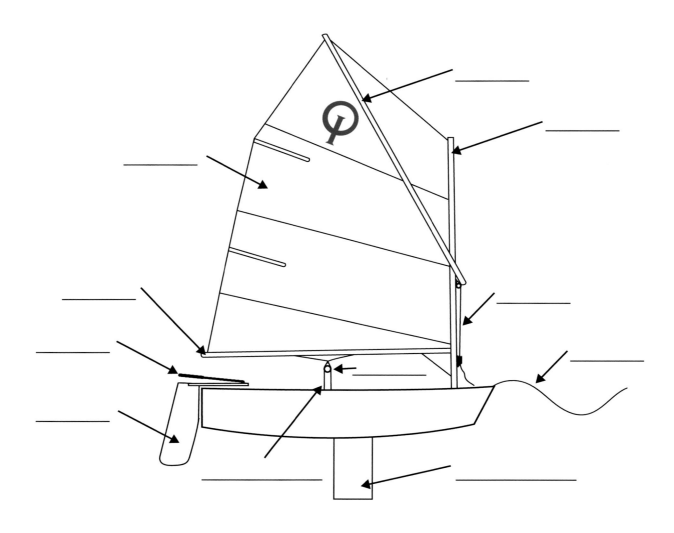

Word Key

Block	Halyard	Rudder
Boom	Mainsail	Sprit
Bowline	Mainsheet	Tiller Extenstion
Daggerboard	Mast	

Optimist Answer Sheet

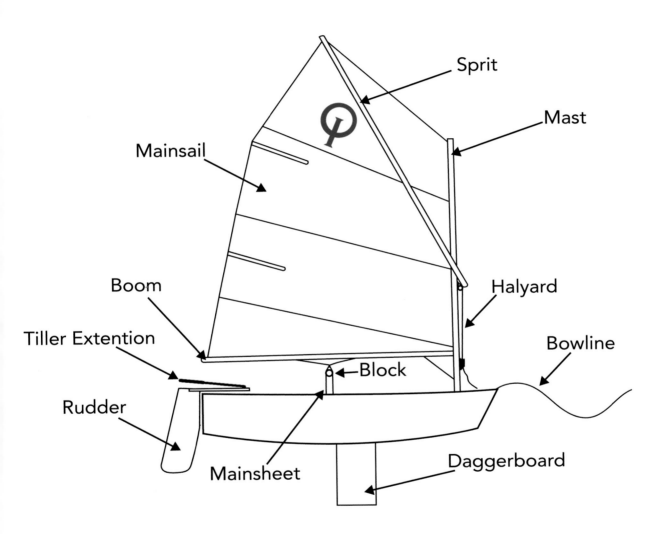

Sprit

Mast

Mainsail

Boom

Halyard

Tiller Extention

Bowline

Rudder

Block

Mainsheet

Daggerboard

RS Feva

Name:_____

Label the boat with the name of the corresponding part.

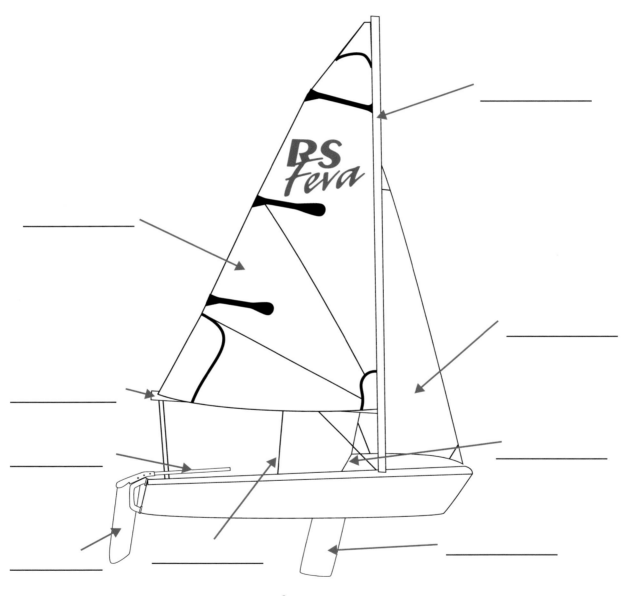

Word Key

Boom	Jib Sheet	Mast
Daggerboard	Mainsail	Rudder
Jib Sail	Mainsheet	Tiller

RS Feva Answer Sheet

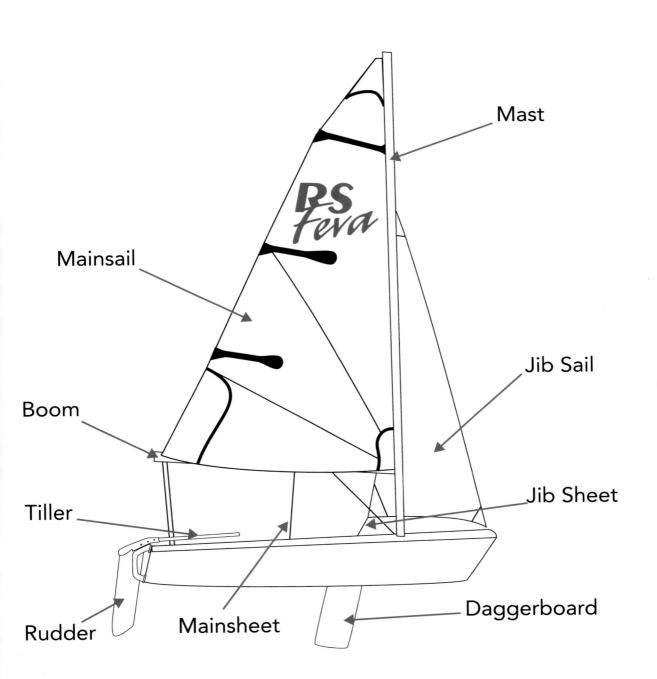

Mast

Mainsail

Jib Sail

Boom

Jib Sheet

Tiller

Rudder

Mainsheet

Daggerboard

Naples Sabot

Name:_____

Label the boat with the name of the corresponding part.

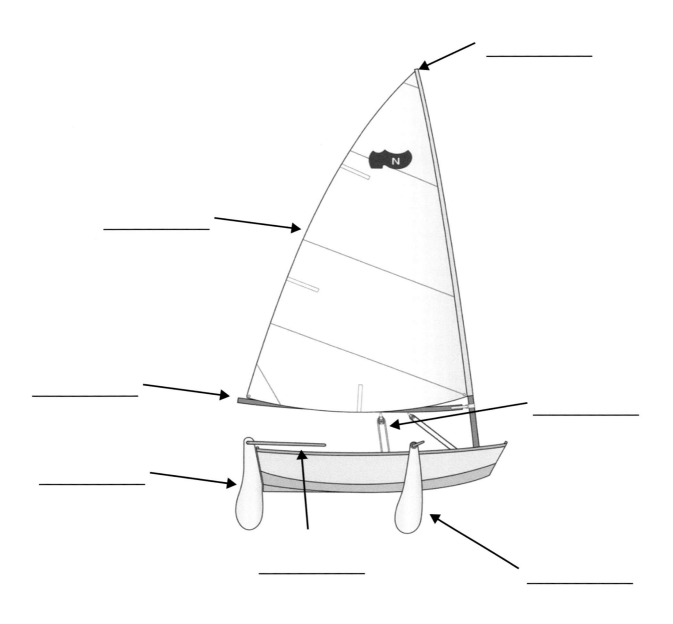

Word Key

Boom	Mainsheet	Tiller
Leeboard	Mast	
Mainsail	Rudder	

Naples Sabot Answer Sheet

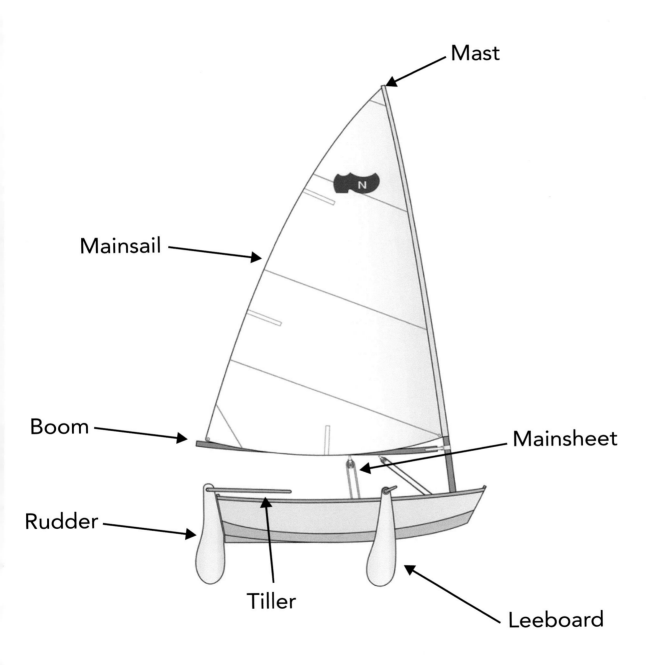

Mast

Mainsail

Boom

Mainsheet

Rudder

Tiller

Leeboard

SONNY ROLLINS OM

For B♭ Instruments • Transcribed Exactly from His Recorded Solos

ISBN 978-1-4950-9286-2

7777 W. BLUEMOUND RD. P.O. BOX 13819 MILWAUKEE, WI 53213

Visit Hal Leonard Online at
www.halleonard.com

WALTER THEODORE "SONNY" ROLLINS

SONNY ROLLINS is the greatest improviser ever! That's what those who love and study his music say. Born September 7, 1930, Sonny has a career that spans nearly the entire history of modern jazz. At the time of this writing, he is 86 and still performing with the legends of jazz.

As a young alto player, I was first introduced to Sonny's music by my improvisation teacher Charlie Shoemake back in the mid 1970s. By using Sonny's transcribed solos, Charlie pointed out to me how Sonny would craft his improvisations following an incredibly well thought out set of musical rules that respected all the important elements of jazz.

Like all accomplished jazz musicians, Sonny studied the greats who preceded him. In particular he adopted the core harmonic approach that Charlie Parker had infused into jazz. With his transcriptions, Charlie Shoemake was able to teach many of the great jazz players of today how to navigate and create their own improvised solos.

Given Charlie's knowledge of Sonny's music, I asked him to hand-select the tunes for this book. These special transcriptions represent the best teaching vessels for the jazz student who is exploring how to improvise. All these transcriptions have been painstakingly created to the best of my ability. I have used a combination of analog and digital manipulation and over forty years of transcribing experience to write down the notes Sonny was playing. You can learn his music and how he approached solo construction from this book with the confidence of minimal errors.

Chris "Doc" Stewart

Here are some words from jazz teacher Charlie Shoemake:

There are three performances by Sonny that I find the most memorable. The first was in 1957 with the Max Roach quintet at a now defunct club called Jazz City. The second was two years later at the same club when he led a trio with bassist Leroy Vinegar and drummer Ron Jefferson. The third appearance was at another long defunct club called The Cloister in 1962 with Jim Hall, Bob Cranshaw, and Ben Riley.

I rank those three experiences as the most inspiring and thrilling jazz playing I have ever heard. He exemplified the most creative, in-depth mastery of the basic three elements of music: melody, rhythm and harmony. Sonny has mastered his craft to the point that his improvisations are completely free of any restriction but still maintain the basic structure of the song. This is to me—though it's a very difficult task and one that requires enormous work—is what truly great jazz playing is supposed to be about. There are numerous great jazz artists whose work the serious student should study, but as another fine contemporary saxophonist (Chris Potter) remarked in an interview, "If you're a saxophonist and you haven't checked out Sonny Rollins...YOU SHOULD DO SO." By studying Sonny Rollins, you will be dealing with not just a portion of the necessary elements of jazz music, but with ALL of them. He has been and always will be a gigantic influence on the way jazz music should be played.

Charlie Shoemake

Airegin

Recorded June 29, 1954 Miles Davis - Bags' Groove (Prestige PRCD-30645)
By Sonny Rollins

All the Things You Are

Recorded November 3, 1957 A Night at the Village Vangaurd (Blue Note 7243 4 99795 2 9)
Lyrics by Oscar Hammerstein II
Music by Jerome Kern

12

Almost Like Being in Love

Recorded October 7, 1953 Sonny Rollins with the Modern Jazz Quartet (Prestige PREP 1337)
Lyrics by Alan Jay Lerner
Music by Frederick Loewe

16

But Not for Me

Recorded June 29, 1954 Miles Davis - Bags' Groove (Prestige PRCD-30645)
Music and Lyrics by George Gershwin and Ira Gershwin

Blue Seven

Recorded June 22, 1956 Saxophone Colossus (Original Jazz Classics OJCCD-291-2)
By Sonny Rollins

Bouncing with Bud

Recorded August 9, 1949 Bud Powell - Bouncing With Bud / Wail (Blue Note 1567)
Words and Music by Earl "Bud" Powell and Walter Gil Fuller

Compulsion

Recorded January 30, 1953 Miles Davis - Collector's Items (Original Jazz Classics OJCCD-071-2)
By Miles Davis

Dance of the Infidels

Recorded August 9, 1949 Fats Navaro - Prime Source (Blue Note BN-LA507-H2)
By Earl "Bud" Powell

Dance of the Infidels

Recorded August 9, 1949 Fats Navaro - Prime Source (Blue Note BN-LA507-H2)
By Earl "Bud" Powell
(Alternate take)

Dig

Recorded October 5, 1951 Miles Davis - Dig (Prestige P-24054)
By Miles Davis

Down

Recorded January 17, 1951 Miles Davis and Horns (Original Jazz Classics OJCCD-053-2)
By Miles Davis

Doxy

Recorded June 29, 1954 Miles Davis - Bags' Groove (Prestige PRCD-30645)
By Sonny Rollins

41

Ev'ry Time We Say Goodbye

Recorded June 11, 1957 Sonny Rollins - The Sound of Sonny (Original Jazz Classics OJCCD-029-2)
Words and Music by Cole Porter

52nd Street Theme

Recorded on August 9, 1949 Fats Navarro - Prime Source (Blue Note BN-LA507-H2)
By Thelonius Monk

47

I Know That You Know

Recorded December 19, 1957 Sonny Side Up (Verve MGV 8262)
Words by Anne Caldwell
Music by Vincent Youmans

I Remember You

Recorded October 5, 1956 Rollins Plays for Bird (Original Jazz Classics OJCCD-214-2)
Words by Johnny Mercer
Music by Victor Schertzinger

Segue into "My Melancholy Baby"

54

I Want to Be Happy

Recorded October 25, 1954 Thelonious Monk and Sonny Rollins (Original Jazz Classics OJCCD-059-2)
Words by Irving Caesar
Music by Vincent Youmans

58

I'll Remember April

Recorded February 17, 1956 Clifford Brown and Max Roach at Basin Street (Verve 314 589 826-2)

Words and Music by Pat Johnston, Don Raye and Gene De Paul

63

65

66

I'll Take Romance

Recorded January 20, 1954 Early Art (Prestige OJCCD-880-2)
Lyrics by Oscar Hammerstein II
Music by Ben Oakland

In Your Own Sweet Way

Recorded March 16, 1956 Miles Davis - Oleo (Prestige PR 7847)

By Dave Brubeck

Just in Time

Recorded June 12, 1957 Sonny Rollins - The Sound of Sonny (Original Jazz Classics OJCCD-029-2)
Words by Betty Comden and Adolph Green
Music by Jule Styne

The Last Time I Saw Paris

Recorded June 19, 1957 Sonny Rollins - The Sound of Sonny (Original Jazz Classics OJCCD-029-2)
Lyrics by Oscar Hammerstein II
Music by Jerome Kern

Mambo Bounce

Recorded December 17, 1951 Sonny Rollins Quartet (Prestige PRLP 137)
By Sonny Rollins

Namely You

Recorded September 22, 1957 Sonny Rollins - Newk's Time (Blue Note CDP 7 84001 2)
Words by Johnny Mercer
Music by Gene De Paul

86

Moving Out

Recorded August 18, 1954 Sonny Rollins - Moving Out (Original Jazz Classics OJCCD-058-2)
By Sonny Rollins

90

No Moe

Recorded October 7, 1953 Sonny Rollins with the Modern Jazz Quartet (Prestige PREP 1337)
By Sonny Rollins

Oleo

Recorded June 29, 1954 Miles Davis - Bags' Groove (Prestige PRCD-30645)
By Sonny Rollins

Old Devil Moon

Recorded November 3, 1957 A Night at the Village Vangaurd (Blue Note 7243 4 99795 2 9)
Words by E.Y. "Yip" Harburg
Music by Burton Lane

Trade 4's with Drums

PLAY 12 X'S GRADUALLY FADING AWAY . . . . .

On a Slow Boat to China

Recorded December 17, 1951 Sonny Rollins with the Modern Jazz Quartet (Prestige PRLP 7029)
By Frank Loesser

Out of the Blue

Recorded October 5, 1951 Miles Davis - Dig (Prestige P-24054)
By Miles Davis

111

Pent Up House

Recorded March 22, 1956 Sonny Rollins Plus 4 (Original Jazz Classics OJCCD-243-2)
By Sonny Rollins

117

Raincheck

Recorded December 2, 1965 Sonny Rollins - Worktime (Original Jazz Classics OJCCD-007-2)
By Billy Strayhorn

St. Thomas

Recorded June 22, 1956 Saxophone Colossus (Original Jazz Classics OJCCD-291-2)
By Sonny Rollins

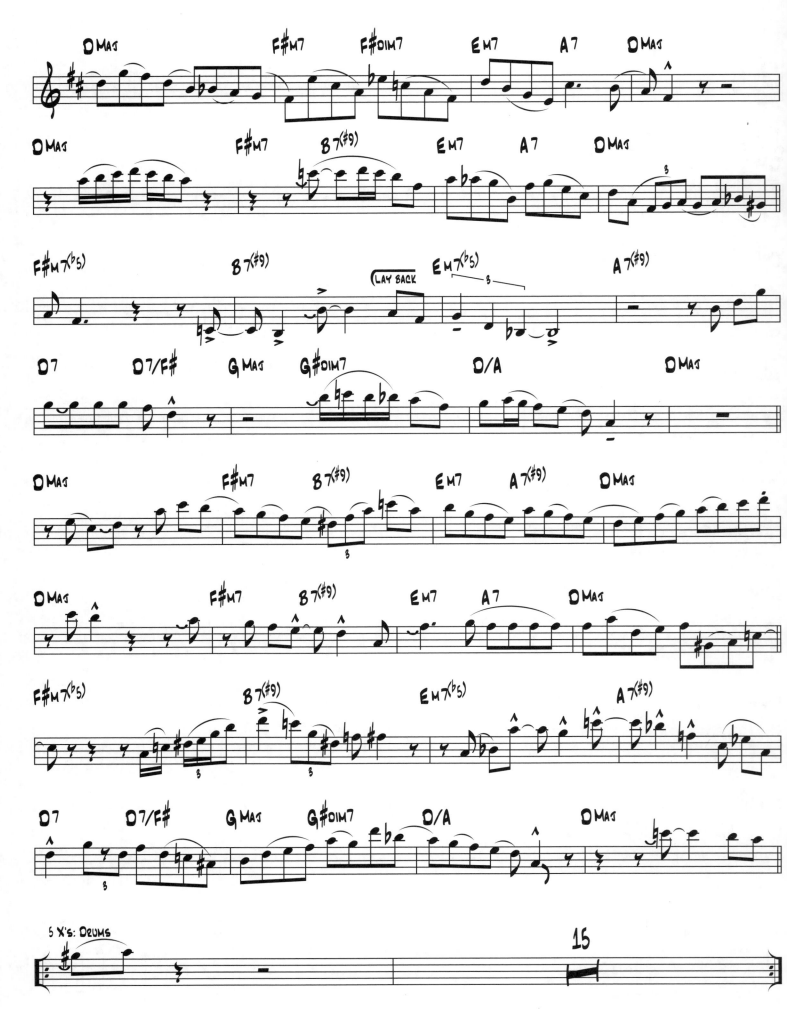

126

128

"You Don't Know What Love Is"

Production ending splice

129

The Scene Is Clean

Recorded February 17, 1956 Clifford Brown and Max Roach at Basin Street (Verve 314 589 826-2)

By Tadd Dameron

131

The Serpent's Tooth

(Take 1)

Recorded January 30, 1953 Miles Davis - Collector's Items (Original Jazz Classics OJCCD-071-2)

By Miles Davis

134

Scoops

Recorded December 17, 1951 Sonny Rollins Quartet (Prestige PRLP 137)
By Sonny Rollins

Solid

Recorded August 18, 1954 Sonny Rollins - Moving Out (Original Jazz Classics OJCCD-058-2)
By Sonny Rollins

140

Sonnymoon For Two

Recorded November 3, 1957 A Night at the Village Vangaurd (Blue Note 7243 4 99795 2 9)
By Sonny Rollins

148

Strode Rode

Recorded June 22, 1956 Saxophone Colossus (Original Jazz Classics OJCCD-291-2)
By Sonny Rollins

Trade 4's with Drums (Skip first 16 bars of tune)

154

156

There Will Never Be Another You

Recorded March 4, 1959 Sonny Rollins Trio in Stockholm 1959 - St Thomas (Dragon DRCD 229)

Lyric by Mack Gordon
Music by Harry Warren

Tenor Madness

Recorded May 24, 1956 Sonny Rollins - Tenor Madness (Original Jazz Classics OJCCD-124-2)
By Sonny Rollins

Toot, Toot, Tootsie (Good-Bye!)

Recorded June 12, 1957 Sonny Rollins - The Sound of Sonny (Original Jazz Classics OJCCD-029-2)

Words and Music by Gus Kahn, Ernie Erdman, Dan Russo and Ted Fiorito

Tune Up

Recorded September 22, 1957 Sonny Rollins - Newk's Time (Blue Note CDP 7 84001 2)
By Miles Davis

MELODY

RUBATO

RHYTHM CUES

F#/E

Valse Hot

Recorded March 22, 1956 Sonny Rollins Plus 4 (Original Jazz Classics OJCCD-243-2)
By Sonny Rollins

Vierd Blues

Recorded March 16, 1956 Miles Davis - Oleo (Prestige PR 7847)
By Miles Davis

Wail

Recorded August 9, 1949 Fats Navarro - Prime Source (Blue Note BN-LA507-H2)
By Earl Powell

What Is This Thing Called Love?

Recorded February 16, 1956 Clifford Brown and Max Roach at Basin Street (Verve 314 589 826-2)

Words and Music by Cole Porter

197

When Your Lover Has Gone

Recorded May 24, 1956 Sonny Rollins - Tenor Madness (Original Jazz Classics OJCCD-124-2)
Words and Music by E.A. Swan

Whispering

Recorded January 17, 1951 Miles Davis and Horns (Original Jazz Classics OJCCD-053-2)
Words and Music by Richard Coburn, John Schonberger and Vincent Rose

Woodyn' You

Recorded September 19, 1956 Max Roach Plus 4 (EmArcy MG 36098)
By Dizzy Gillespie

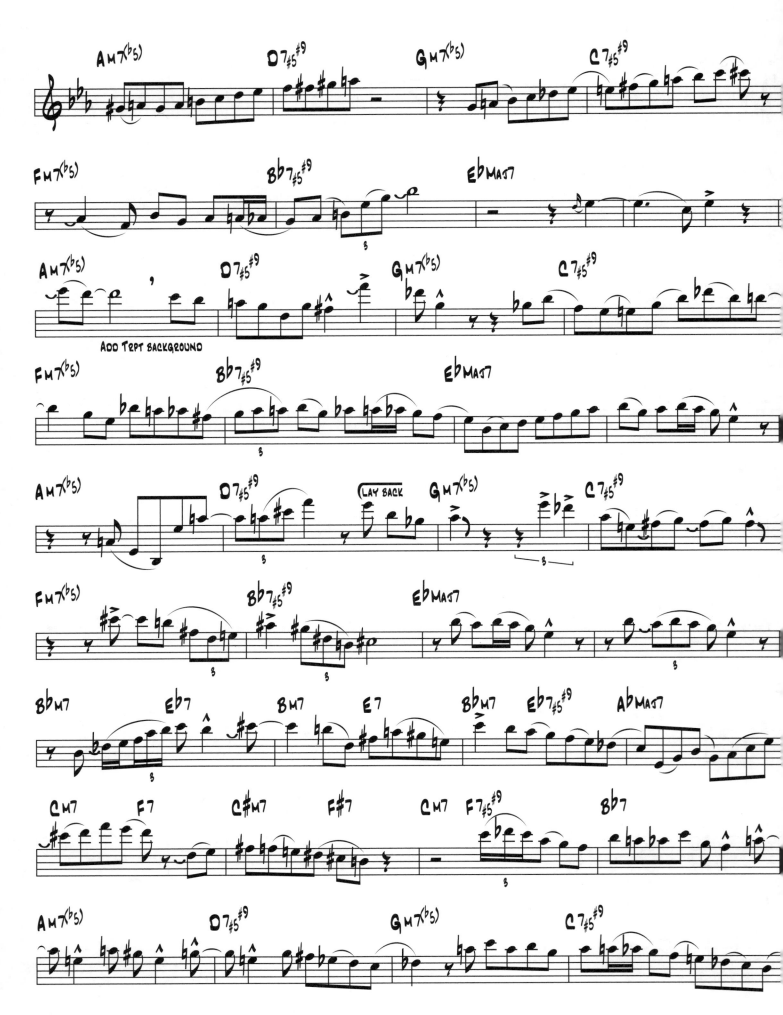

You Stepped Out of Dream

Recorded April 15, 1957 Sonny Rollins - Volume 2 (Blue Note BLP 1558)
Words by Gus Kahn
Music by Nacio Herb Brown

211

SAXOPHONE
IMPROVE YOUR TECHNIQUE

AMAZING PHRASING
50 WAYS TO IMPROVE YOUR IMPROVISATIONAL SKILLS
by Dennis Taylor

Amazing Phrasing is for any sax player interested in learning how to improvise and how to improve their creative phrasing. The ideas are divided into three sections: harmony, rhythm, and melody. The companion audio includes full-band tracks in various musical styles for listening and play along.

00311108 Alto Sax, Book/CD Pack............... $17.99
00310787 Tenor Sax, Book/Online Audio...... $16.99

PAUL DESMOND
A STEP-BY-STEP BREAKDOWN OF THE SAX STYLES AND TECHNIQUES OF A JAZZ GREAT
by Eric J. Morones

Examine the sophisticated sounds of a jazz sax legend with this instructional pack that explores 12 Desmond classics: Alone Together • Any Other Time • Bossa Antigua • I've Got You Under My Skin • Jazzabelle • Take Five • Take Ten • Time After Time • and more.
00695983 Book/CD Pack............................ $19.99

JAZZ SAXOPHONE
AN IN-DEPTH LOOK AT THE STYLES OF THE TENOR MASTERS
by Dennis Taylor

All the best are here: from the cool bebop excursions of Dexter Gordon, to the stellar musings of John Coltrane, with more than a dozen master players examined in between. Includes lessons, music, historical analysis and rare photos, plus a CD with 16 full-band tracks!
00310983 Book/CD Pack............................ $18.95

MODERN SAXOPHONE TECHNIQUES
by Frank Catalano

Many books present facts, but this guude teaches the developing player how to learn. Listening, exploring, writing original music, and trial and error are some of the methods threaded throughout. On the online video, author and virtuoso saxophonist Frank Catalano offers quick tips on many of the topics covered in the book. Topics include: developing good rhythm • air stream and embouchure • fingering charts • tonguing techniques • modern harmony tips • and more.
00123829 Book/Online Video...................... $24.99

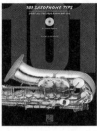

101 SAXOPHONE TIPS
by Eric Morones

This book presents valuable how-to insight that saxophone players of all styles and levels can benefit from. The text, photos, music, diagrams, and accompanying CD provide a terrific, easy-to-use resource for a variety of topics, including: techniques; maintenance; equipment; practicing; recording; performance; and much more!
00311082 Book/CD Pack............................ $15.99

SONNY ROLLINS
A STEP-BY-STEP BREAKDOWN OF THE SAX STYLES & TECHNIQUES OF A JAZZ GIANT

Explore the unique sound and soul of jazz innovator Sonny Rollins on licks from 12 classic songs: Airegin • Biji • Don't Stop the Carnival • Doxy • Duke of Iron • God Bless' the Child • Oleo • St. Thomas • Sonnymoon for Two • Tenor Madness • Way Out West • You Don't Know What Love Is.
00695854 Book/CD Pack............................ $19.99

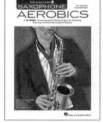

SAXOPHONE AEROBICS
by Woody Mankowski

This 52-week, one-exercise-a-day workout program for developing, improving and maintaining saxophone technique includes access to demo audio tracks online for all 365 workout licks! Techniques covered include: scales • articulations • rhythms • range extension • arpeggios • ornaments • and stylings. Benefits of using this book include: facile technique • better intonation • increased style vocabulary • heightened rhythmic acuity • improved ensemble playing • and expanded range.
00143344 Book/Online Audio...................... $19.99

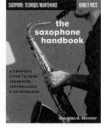

THE SAXOPHONE HANDBOOK
COMPLETE GUIDE TO TONE, TECHNIQUE, AND PERFORMANCE
by Douglas D. Skinner
Berklee Press

A complete guide to playing and maintenance, this handbook offers essential information on all dimensions of the saxophone. It provides an overview of technique, such as breathing, fingerings, articulations, and more. Exercises will help you develop your sense of timing, facility, and sound. You'll learn to fine-tune your reed, recork the keys, fix binding keys, replace pads, and many other repairs and adjustments. You'll also learn to improve your tone, intonation, and flexibility while playing with proper technique.
50449658 .... $14.99

SAXOPHONE SOUND EFFECTS
by Ueli Dörig
Berklee Press

Add unique saxophone sounds to your palette of colors! The saxophone is capable of a great range of sounds, from laughs and growls to multiphonics and percussion effects. This book shows you how to do 19 different inventive effects, with etudes that put them in a musical context. The accompanying online audio provides play-along tracks for the etudes and examples of each sound effect in isolation.
50449628 Book/Online Audio...................... $15.99

SAXOPHONE WORKOUT
by Eric J. Morones

This book will give you a complete saxophone workout. Here you'll find etudes that cover a wide spectrum of techniques, from the basics to intermeidate level to advanced. With daily practice that includes use of a metronome and tuner, this book will provide noticeable improvement in the mastery of your horn. The excercises are designed for the trouble spots of all the instruments of the saxophone family – soprano, alto, tenor, baritone – and can be used by players at all levels.
00121478 .... $12.99

25 GREAT SAX SOLOS
TRANSCRIPTIONS • LESSONS • BIOS • PHOTOS
by Eric J. Morones

From Chuck Rio and King Curtis to David Sanborn and Kenny G, take an inside look at the genesis of pop saxophone. This book with online audio provides solo transcriptions in standard notation, lessons on how to play them, bios, equipment, photos, history, and much more. The audio contains full-band demos of every sax solo in the book, and includes the PLAYBACK+ audio player which allows you to adjust the recording to any tempo without changing pitch, loop challenging parts, pan, and more! Songs include: After the Love Has Gone • Deacon Blues • Just the Two of Us • Just the Way You Are • Mercy, Mercy Me • Money • Respect • Spooky • Take Five • Tequila • Yakety Sax • and more.
00311315 Book/Online Audio...................... $19.99

HAL•LEONARD
www.halleonard.com

Prices, content, and availability subject to change without notice.

0118